# Cambridge Elements ≡

Elements in Anthropological Archaeology in the 21st Century
edited by
Eli Dollarhide
*New York University Abu Dhabi*
Michael Galaty
*University of Michigan*
Junko Habu
*University of California, Berkeley*
Patricia A. McAnany
*University of North Carolina at Chapel Hill*
John K. Millhauser
*North Carolina State University*
Rita Wright
*New York University*

T0328675

# COLLECTIVE ACTION AND THE REFRAMING OF EARLY MESOAMERICA

David M. Carballo
*Boston University*

Gary M. Feinman
*Field Museum of Natural History*

CAMBRIDGE
UNIVERSITY PRESS

Shaftesbury Road, Cambridge CB2 8EA, United Kingdom

One Liberty Plaza, 20th Floor, New York, NY 10006, USA

477 Williamstown Road, Port Melbourne, VIC 3207, Australia

314–321, 3rd Floor, Plot 3, Splendor Forum, Jasola District Centre,
New Delhi – 110025, India

103 Penang Road, #05–06/07, Visioncrest Commercial, Singapore 238467

Cambridge University Press is part of Cambridge University Press & Assessment,
a department of the University of Cambridge.

We share the University's mission to contribute to society through the pursuit of
education, learning and research at the highest international levels of excellence.

www.cambridge.org
Information on this title: www.cambridge.org/9781009476027

DOI: 10.1017/9781009338677

First published 2023

*A catalogue record for this publication is available from the British Library*

ISBN 978-1-009-47602-7 Hardback
ISBN 978-1-009-33870-7 Paperback
ISSN 2753-6327 (online)
ISSN 2753-6319 (print)

Cambridge University Press & Assessment has no responsibility for the persistence
or accuracy of URLs for external or third-party internet websites referred to in this
publication and does not guarantee that any content on such websites is, or will
remain, accurate or appropriate.

# Collective Action and the Reframing of Early Mesoamerica

Elements in Anthropological Archaeology in the 21st Century

DOI: 10.1017/9781009338677
First published online: December 2023

David M. Carballo
*Boston University*

Gary M. Feinman
*Field Museum of Natural History*

**Author for correspondence:** David M. Carballo, carballo@bu.edu

**Abstract:** In considering the long trajectory of human societies, researchers have too often favored models of despotic control by the few or structural models that fail to grant agency to those with less power in shaping history. Recent scholarship demonstrates such models to be not only limiting but also empirically inaccurate. This Element reviews archaeological approaches to collective action drawing on theoretical perspectives from across the globe and case studies from prehispanic Mesoamerica. It highlights how institutions and systems of governance matter, vary over space and time, and can oscillate between more pluralistic and more autocratic forms within the same society, culture, or polity. The historical coverage examines resource dilemmas and ways of mediating them, how ritual and religion can foster both social solidarity and hierarchy, the political financing of institutions and variability in forms of governance, and lessons drawn to inform the building of more resilient communities in the present.

**Keywords:** archaeology, Mesoamerica, collective action, governance, Aztecs

ISBNs: 9781009476027 (HB), 9781009338707 (PB), 9781009338677 (OC)
ISSNs: 2753-6327 (online), 2753-6319 (print)

# Contents

# 1 Working Together: Theoretical Approaches and Historical Cases of Collective Action

One of the great challenges of our time is to understand and promote ways that people can work cooperatively and collectively towards shared goals. This is a long-standing and enduring challenge that some of the earliest social theorists grappled with. Nonetheless, our definitions of shared goals and our strategies for pursuing them vary culturally and through time. In our globalized present, the most pressing concerns operate at the planetary scale of climate change mitigation, international nuclear treaties, infectious disease pandemics, and others that affect sustaining life on Earth as we know it. In the grand scope of human history, these are concerns we have only realized relatively recently. Others have consumed humans for millennia yet are still relevant today and establish the foundations for addressing global challenges – concerns such as making a living and providing for one's family or more extended kin networks; getting along with and making shared decisions with neighbors regarding our neighborhoods, towns, and cities; or creating and sustaining societal norms and institutions that are generally trusted and provide a widely shared sense of being well governed. For these, we possess a historical and archaeological record attesting to relative successes and failures that can inform us about how we should be working towards them today at similar, nested scales of supra-household groups, neighborhoods, settlements, polities, and even larger worlds made up of multiple political units. Examinations of past cases can help inform our thinking regarding how to address the really big global issues that we face from the bottom-up, working with community networks that we are most familiar with and most closely connected to.

Here we set out to consider a suite of interdisciplinary frameworks for how and why people work together to manage resources, cooperate as groups larger than families, and sustain governing institutions that are relatively trusted and more pluralistic, meaning providing a voice in decision-making to more people. We draw on cases from different parts of the world to illustrate key concepts so that they could apply to considerations of societal organization in any particular region or time period. In subsequent sections we narrow our focus to Mesoamerica, as a suite of case studies we know best, in order to outline the concepts more fully and apply them more concretely to specific social institutions and archaeological contexts.

## 1.1 Resource Management and the Commons

Since we are examining issues of collective action in the archaeological and historical record, we thought it appropriate to start off with a utilitarian artifact. Figure 1 depicts a cowbell. It is not the sort of relic from the past that gets

**Figure 1** Photo of a cowbell recovered from an excavation at Boston Common and dating to ca. 1770–1830, when the common could be used for grazing animals. Used with permission from Bagley (2016).

romanticized by popular media, but this cowbell tells a story that connects with bigger issues of how societies organize themselves. It was discovered in Boston Common during a 1987 archaeological survey and likely dates between 1770 and 1830 (Bagley 2016: 113–114, 131–133). The later date provides what archaeologists call a *terminus post quem*, or limit after which the cowbell could reasonably date to, because 1830 is when Boston decreed the Common to be a public park, prohibiting residents from grazing their animals on it. For almost two centuries prior, starting in 1634, Boston Common had been set aside for communal pastureland, as well as less bucolic uses such as storing munitions in the town's powder house and the occasional public execution, including of women accused of witchcraft. In the early years of Boston Common, its use for grazing was restricted to adult white males and overuse during its first decade led to a town ordinance on how many animals could graze, limiting an owner to one cow or four sheep at a time.

Commons of this sort were, well, common in England too and had been transposed to Boston and other North American settlements by Anglo colonists. Soon after Bostonians outlawed grazing on Boston Common, the English author William Forster Lloyd (1833) published two lectures using a parable of the commons titled *Two Lectures on the Checks to Population*. Lloyd noted the tensions between individual and group interests inherent to managing shared resources, as it is in any single person's interest to use a resource as much as possible, but it is in the group's interest that the resource not be overexploited – or overgrazed, in this particular case. Lloyd's parable was revived and popularized more than a century later as the "tragedy of the commons" by the American ecologist Garrett Hardin (1968), who reflected three decades later that he should have been more specific in branding it a "tragedy of unmanaged commons" (Hardin 1998). Although Hardin's popular coinage for communal resource management has been very influential, his proposed solutions were immoral as he espoused white nationalist and anti-immigrant ideas as the means of managing the commons (Mildenberger 2019). Hardin's notions of who among a population actually gets to use the commons were not much different than those of the settler colonists of three centuries earlier.

What we consider abstractly as "the commons" is therefore subject to societal dynamics of governance, social inequality, definitions of in-groups versus out-groups, and related factors. This has been particularly well illustrated by the recent work of Heather McGhee (2021), who examines how the intersection of racism and classism in the United States has historically undermined collective action in managing common-pool resources, including, most evocatively and literally, in access to public spaces such as community swimming pools. These cultural, historical, and societal factors defining inclusion and exclusion can be among the most determinative in how individuals define themselves as groups and whether they do or do not cooperate with one another.

Since its elaboration as a coherent body of theory in the 1960s by scholars such as Mancur Olson (1965), collective action theory has offered a productive, interdisciplinary framework for explaining how and why people act out of selfish interests or as contingent cooperators and how that affects who has access to particular resource systems. We are partial to the work of Elinor Ostrom (e.g., 1990, 1998, 2000, 2005, 2007), the first woman to be awarded the Nobel Prize in economics, as she skillfully bridged multiscalar levels of analyses, from elegant yet abstract mathematical models derived from game theory to the thick description of how irrigation and other resource management systems work on the ground, drawing from actual ethnographic and historical cases. Ostrom and colleagues (1994) developed an organizational framework for classifying types of goods, resource systems, and the cooperation dilemmas that may arise from misalignments between individual and group interests or from asymmetries in power (see also Ostrom 2005: 24–26). In Figure 2, we elaborate on the simple graphic schema they developed to illustrate these points with a sampling of examples that are often considered in archaeological discussions of managing land and other resources (e.g., Bayman and Sullivan 2008; Blanton and Fargher 2008; Carballo and Feinman 2016; Eerkens 1999; Kohler 1992; Oosthuizen 2013).

The representation is only schematic, and the arrows in Figure 2 are intended to indicate how any type of good or resource could vary depending on factors

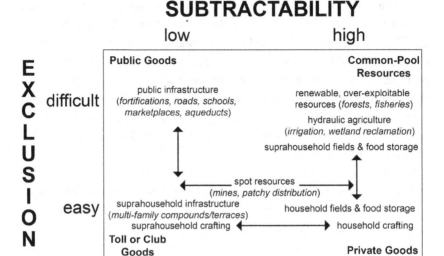

**Figure 2** Text box schema presenting a classification of goods and resource systems, based on Ostrom and colleagues (1994), with examples of infrastructure and management strategies frequently discussed by archaeologists.

The two major axes for classification are the subtractability of a resource, meaning how much people using it depletes the resource, and its potential for excluding others from using it.

beyond ecology and economy, especially cultural, social, or historical ones. In general, we might consider a spectrum from fully public to fully private resources that reflects how easy it is for an individual or small group of people to exclude others from that resource – the exclusion axis on the left. But the framework also considers the scale of the resource – the subtractability axis on top – and the degree to which any use of it impacts others doing so as well. Resources with high subtractability are more finite than resources with low subtractability, such as energy from fossil fuels versus solar power. Their higher susceptibility to over-exploitation is why so much attention has been given to investigating common-pool resources (CPRs, in this literature). Management of common-pool resources among ancestral populations who primarily hunted, fished, or collected foods (i.e., "hunter-gatherers" or "fisher-foragers") includes examples from the Southeastern United States, where rich ecosystems permitted seasonal or permanent sedentism on the part of relatively large populations (Thompson 2022). Since these subsistence resources were not privatized and were subtractable, they present common-pool resource problems analogous to contemporary management of the same – such as preventing the overexploitation of game species, fisheries, and forests (Acheson 2011, 2015). Although global populations have vastly increased, and our exploitation of such resources has been mechanized and industrialized, the basic logic of collective action remains the same: in any given social-ecological system, how resources are classed and managed derives from interactions between different nested scales of resources, users, and governing structures (Andersson and Ostrom 2008; Ostrom 2009).

## 1.2 Governance and Fiscal Systems

To provide other examples of the sorts of resource issues outlined in Section 1.1 and their intersection with governing structures, let us consider the hypothetical example of an agricultural society where successful farming is based on receiving adequate rainfall. In a fully rainfed system, rainwater could be classed as a public good since it falls equally on everyone's field and does not exclude anyone or subtract from the possibility of it going somewhere else. Yet if this same society devises an irrigation network to channelize rainwater towards particular fields, that network could now be classed as a common-pool resource and governing structures relating to how the irrigation canals and associated fields are managed (i.e., centrally vs. locally, collectively vs. privately) become the key variable in understanding how resource management was organized. Governing systems can impact the full spectrum of resource systems, not simply common-pool resources. Within public goods we list examples mostly drawn from the built environment and urban infrastructure, assuming high access among a population. Yet an aqueduct designed to bring water to a palace rather than a wider public would, in contrast, be classed at the other end of a spectrum as a private good. Alternatively, if the use of a public good were somehow governed by expectations that users participated in its construction or maintenance, there could be social mechanisms to exclude those who did not contribute – termed "free riders" in this literature – from enjoying the benefit. Sanctions for such transgression could range from light and informal measures, like gossip or shaming, to formal ostracism from the group or even death (Boehm 2012: 84–87; Carballo 2013a: 11–13; Ostrom 1990: 94–100).

Spot resources, listed roughly in the middle of the chart, are easier to exclude others from obtaining than are those with wide distribution and could even be monopolized by a few individuals or small, powerful groups, classing them as private goods or toll/club goods. On their own, the management of spot resources offers dilemmas that social scientists usually find less interesting to probe, but not when they are part of the fiscal systems of governing institutions. These relationships were examined in comparative, historical perspective by the political scientist Margaret Levi (1988) and were elaborated from historical premodern states by the archaeologists Richard Blanton and Lane Fargher (2008) in considering the relationships between fiscal streams and systems of governance more broadly. Their detailed analyses of comparative cases demonstrate that a key factor determining variability in the organization of large-scale societies is whether revenues are largely internal (more communal and widely available resources) or external (such as spot resources, often coming from long distances, but also war booty, tenant rent, and toll taxes on long-distance trade). This axis of political-economic variability is also classified as a spectrum between inclusive and extractive political institutions (Acemoglu and Robinson 2012). It is a relatively simple distinction that has major consequences for the levels of accountability that leaders face from the populace at large and the likelihood that governance and power will be shared versus individualized (Blanton and Fargher 2008: 114–132, 2016: 106–114). In addition to greater accountability for political elites, higher levels of internal financing and communal resources tend to be positively correlated with higher dissemination of public goods and bureaucratization of civic offices, together creating systems that may grow larger and be more resilient to social perturbations than more autocratic or despotic formations (Blanton and Fargher 2016; Feinman and Carballo 2018).

An important point to emphasize here is that collective action operates at multiple social scales – ranging from cooperating households to the political alliances of large states (Birch 2022) – and while the particular forms of collective action characteristic of any particular society shape the broad contours of societal organization, they are not immutable (Arroyo Abad and Maurer 2021). In fact, they change frequently as individuals and groups strategize their actions in association with shifting socioeconomic variables and historical contingencies. Human decisions to shift their social norms and levels of trust in institutions, as well as in the variable arrangements for financing governance, have profound cumulative effects for broader societal organization. We can draw from two canonical works of anthropology to illustrate the types of mechanisms by which such variability and change can occur. In the classic work of political anthropology *Political Systems of Highland Burma*, Edmund Leach (1954) developed a model for Kachin social organization that involved oscillations between a more egalitarian and pluralistic structure (*gumlao*) and a more hierarchical and exclusionary structure (*gumsa*).

> In brief, the *gumsa* conceive of themselves as being ruled by chiefs who are members of an hereditary aristocracy; the *gumlao* repudiate all notions of hereditary class difference. *Gumsa* regard *gumlao* as commoner serfs who

have revolted against their lawful masters; *gumlao* regard *gumsa* as tyrants and snobs. But while the two terms represent in Kachin thinking two fundamentally opposed modes of organization, both are consistent with the same general set of cultural trappings which we recognize as Kachin. (Leach 1977: 198)

Leach's work was important in showing the possibility for political variability and change among people with strongly shared cultural norms. He illustrated how relatively minor changes in ritual practices could be a major driver of this variability. For instance, within gumsa groups a chief was entitled to conduct major sacrifices, promote supernatural entities associated with his lineage over those of others, and pass his ritual powers off to sons, whereas such initiatives were more distributed, community responsibilities in gumlao groups, who prioritized loyalty to place over lineage. Since Leach's study, the reasons for variability and change in Kachin groups along the gumlao/gumsa spectrum have been debated by scholars, with some arguing that more egalitarian organization was the result of Kachin chiefs losing the external fiscal streams (in opium, enslaved peoples, and taxes extracted on trade caravans and as a protection racket) that underwrote their power and others arguing that egalitarianism was a conscious choice made by particular groups in strategic opposition to the hierarchical states (the Shan and the English) within their broader sphere of interaction (Nugent 1982; Robinne and Sadan 2007; Scott 2009).

This second explanation, of definition in purposeful opposition to another, recalls the yet earlier canonical work in anthropology by Gregory Bateson, who in *Naven* (1936; see also Bateson 1935) elaborated the concept of "schismogenesis" as the process by which individuals in a society might progressively differentiate themselves, thereby creating schisms with others. Like with the gumlao/gumsa oscillations, schismogenesis provides a heuristic tool for thinking about purposeful and agentive change, rather than envisioning particular social "types" to be fixed or inevitable due to external ecological factors or power dynamics. The concept has also been applied to entire cultures in contact, with examples from classical antiquity such as democratic Athenians versus oligarchic Spartans or, more broadly, pluralistic Greeks versus autocratic Persians (Graeber and Wengrow 2021: 56–58, 180). If considered as a process of divergent ethnogenesis, schismogenesis has value in considering ideational mechanisms that can lead to the definition of in- and out-groups structuring conflicts over more material concerns, such as resource management. For instance, it has been used to describe progressive differentiation leading to factional conflicts over common-pool resources, including salmon fisheries among Native populations of the Pacific Northwest (Harrison and Loring 2014), connecting back to issues of resource management (see also Blanton 2015; Feinman 2022).

The interactions between people, resources, and governing structures therefore have great explanatory value in considering variability and change in societal organization in the deep past. Archaeology offers a material lens on these issues and a diachronic, deep-time perspective on the resources people used and their identification as part of polities, settlements, ethnic or religious groups, gender or age divisions, households, and even sometimes as individuals. A challenge is how to identify governance archaeologically, including what Holland-Lulewicz and colleagues (2022) term the "keystone institutions" that promote and sustain collective action and more pluralistic governance.

## 1.3 Institutions, Infrastructure, and the Archaeological Record

Because archaeology engages primarily with a material record of the past, the sorts of undertakings that people may have worked more or less collectively towards are interpreted largely through elements of the built environment such as architecture and infrastructure, the relative distributions of economic goods, and imagery that may convey past ideas about human relations among one another and with supernatural entities (Blanton and Fargher 2016; Carballo 2013c; Stanish 2017). These material remains are widespread across the globe, but determining the cultural institutions that promoted and organized them can be more challenging as, "[b]roadly defined, institutions are the prescriptions that humans use to organize all forms of repetitive and structured interactions including those within families, neighborhoods, markets, firms, sports leagues, churches, private associations, and governments at all scales" Ostrom (2005: 3). Although the term often implies formality or rigidity, as in their imposition by powerful groups, we adopt a broad definition of institutions in this Element because anthropologists and other social scientists have demonstrated how they can form through more organic, bottom-up processes of repeated interactions by individuals adhering to widely agreed upon cultural norms and rules (Glowacki 2020). Being cultural templates or prescriptions for behavior, understanding the institutions of past societies usually requires textual evidence from the period, historical connections drawing on oral histories and contemporary practices of descendant communities, or judicious analogy with cases that appear similar in related institutions. Interpretations based on the first two lines of evidence tend to be more compelling than those based on the third since they are grounded in the cultural logic of a given society.

Today we often think of infrastructure in relation to cities or the transportation networks that link urban areas together. Yet a recent emphasis on "green infrastructure" in cities, usually meaning green spaces like parks or environmental mitigation strategies in response to climate change, articulates with a much longer history of managing ecologies for subsistence through a human built environment – and we are not the only species to do so, as beaver dams, termite mounds, and other nonhuman built environments attest to (Barua 2021). A broader archaeological definition of infrastructure could include its materialization of some sort of consensus undertaking between people through "the manifestation of multi-user physical networks" (Smith 2016: 165). Though these arrangements certainly ramped up with more "users" living near one another on a permanent basis (Feinman and Neitzel 2023), they can also be seen among mobile foraging populations. In fact, some of the earliest subsistence infrastructure anywhere in the world could be said to be the desert kites of Pre-Pottery Neolithic B (PPNB) in southwest Asia – large linear stone formations that PPNB hunters began constructing and depicting in engraved-stone monuments some 9,000 years ago as communal hunting strategies to funnel herds of gazelles, aurochs, and other species to specific kill zones or pit traps (Crassard et al. 2022, 2023). Zooarchaeological remains and human-animal imagery in the sculpture from Göbekli Tepe and other sites in southeastern Turkey, representing some of the earliest documented large communal structures in the world, connect this type of collective construction to public architecture and monumental sculpture of early religious traditions (Pöllath et al. 2018). Similar features of stone lanes for driving large migratory animals such as caribou were constructed by groups of cooperating hunters in North America at least 9,000 years ago (O'Shea et al. 2014). Large fish weirs are in a sense the aquatic parallel to these sorts of terrestrial features and allow for the corralling of fish for easy spearing and netting. Their construction among fisher-forager populations such as Florida's Calusa represents a related form of collective subsistence infrastructure (Thompson et al. 2018).

Cases of communal hunting and fisheries management such as these have been productive lines of analysis for collective action relating to common-pool resources and how its organization articulated with cultural norms and institutions. Among agricultural populations, investment in subsistence infrastructure continued or intensified, with the construction of networks of terraces, irrigation canals, reservoirs, wetland raised fields, and others that would fit in the schematic of Figure 2 representing forms of landesque capital or sunk costs in the built environment whose construction and maintenance generate long-term economic dividends if cooperative arrangements can be sustained (Feinman et al. 2023; Widgren 2007).

And how were cooperative arrangements sustained? Through the archaeological record we can see a few pathways that operate at different social scales and implicate different forms of archaeological data: one set relating more to space (i.e., architecture and the built environment), from supra-household groups like corporate houses or neighborhoods to public arenas for gathering, ritual, and performance; and one set relating more to things (i.e., artifact and ecofact distributions, household assemblages, or mortuary deposits) bearing on levels of social inequality and the fiscal underpinning of power relations. We will examine these two broad sets of data in turn, along with the interpretations archaeologists have drawn from them regarding collective action.

The first, more spatial dimension to sustaining cooperation dovetails with a large literature in the social and behavioral sciences on mutual monitoring – the shared understanding generated when people are able to keep track of one another and evaluate their level of participation in and commitment to collective undertakings, leading them to trust that a given system is "fair" (e.g., Bowles and Gintis 2002; Chwe 2001; Ostrom et al. 2003).

> [M]ost long-surviving resource regimes select their own monitors, who are accountable to the users or are users themselves and who keep an eye on resource conditions as well as on user behavior ... Conditional cooperation and mutual monitoring reinforce one another, especially in regimes where the rules are designed to reduce monitoring costs. Over time, further adherence to shared norms evolves and high levels of cooperation are achieved without the need to engage in very close and costly monitoring to enforce rule conformance. (Ostrom 2000: 151–152)

One means of reducing the costs of monitoring is to have multiple families live together in exceptionally large houses featuring continual interaction and shared domestic tasks capable of creating scalar economies within the confines of shared residential walls (Banning and Coupland 1996; Hirth 2020: 22–23, 36–38). These will naturally have limits on their total size, but some "big house" traditions featured residences that could accommodate several dozens to low hundreds of people. At the larger scales of neighborhood or entire settlements, the costs of monitoring could be achieved through integrative public ritual and the ritualization of collective work (Stanish 2017). Here, elements of the built environment such as open plazas or courtyards could provide venues to organize and incentivize participation in collective endeavors through work feasts or public recognition. The archaeological record is full of plazas and communal architecture that could be interpreted as integrative, but it is important to consider other contextual information because these settings can also be used for public performance of inequality and displays of hierarchy (Dungan and Peebles 2018; Feinman 2016; Fisher 2009; Inomata 2006). Open plazas could just as easily be used for pluralistic purposes of public assembly and lively political debate (the classical Athenian Agora) as for displays of autocratic rule and squashing dissent (Beijing's Tiananmen Square in the late twentieth century). Likewise, all pyramidal type monumental architecture was not created for the same reasons, and those that were built as mortuary complexes for divine rulers or to extoll the virtues of a dynasty clearly projected more exclusive and unequal symbolism than those built in honor of widely venerated deities or broad cosmological principles. Levels of access, related symbolism, and other cues to how such public spaces were actually used are therefore critical to their analysis and interpretation.

Another important subset of the built environment are spaces created or set aside for purposeful deliberation in a more pluralistic, rather than autocratic, system of governance. These can also vary greatly by culture and through time so require other lines of information other than spatial ones to determine their uses. For instance, because of a rich textual record and well-preserved architectural remains, we can see tiers of democratic decision-making in the urban plans of classical Greek poleis centers, such as dedicated council houses (bouleuterion) adjacent to the open and multifunctional agora, but with restricted access and seating for a council that would deliberate on items to present at a larger popular assembly (ekklesia) that may need to meet at the town's theater (Paga 2017; Small 2009). The openness of the agora and semicircular seating of the council and theater buildings were conducive to a spectrum of political discourse among those defined as citizens. Other spaces for pluralistic assembly might be hard to detect in the absence of texts because of their minimal modification or architectural elaboration, such as the Germanic *thing* and later progeny in the Icelandic Althing (Thurston 2022). The construction of more elaborate, centrally located architecture with high accessibility may serve as a spatial cue for deliberative spaces in context that lack supporting texts, as has been proposed for colonnaded structures in cities of the Indus Valley civilization (Green 2022). For cases lacking textual documentation, it is also difficult to discern who were able to participate in political discourse within deliberative spaces and how a society defined in-groups and out-groups. Comparative studies of Greek and Roman political history highlight another axis of variability in the inclusion/exclusion of people defined as citizens, with the first having defined this in-group more restrictively but empowered those select few with decision-making abilities in a more pluralistic system of governance, while the second defined citizens more inclusively, particularly with imperial growth, but as part of a less pluralistic system of governance (Rhodes 2009).

In some cases, early institutions of more pluralistic governance can be gleaned from triangulating between the known institutions of later sources and the archaeological record. Such is the case for council houses in the Southeastern United States, where Native peoples such as the Muskogee have centuries of documented use of these deliberative spaces and can be identified archaeologically dating back some 1,500 years at Ancestral Muskogean sites (Holland-Lulewictz et al. 2022; Thompson et al. 2022). The largest council houses measure more than 35 m in diameter and could have held hundreds of people, not unlike the bouleuterion of classical Greek democratic instructions. A smaller but particularly well-preserved example was discovered nearly a century ago at Ocmulgee in central Georgia (also known as Macon Mounds), which was identified both as an "earth lodge" and as a "council chamber" during the national collective labor projects of New Deal archaeology (Fairbanks 1946; Kelly 1938). The circular structure was well preserved, with burnt timbers from the roof covering a packed clay floor some 13 m in diameter with a bench running along the circumference that becomes progressively lower towards the entrance from a platform depicting a raptorial bird with a forked-eye motif – a trait characteristic of peregrine falcons, admired as the animal capable of the fastest speeds in the world (Byers 1962) (Figure 3). Featuring forty-seven seats along the bench and spaces for another three on the falcon platform, the structure was designed to seat fifty people in a manner that simultaneously expressed some social hierarchy in spatial proximity to the platform versus the entrance but also in a spatial arrangement designed to ensure mutual visibility and allow for group deliberation. The structure is therefore a wonderful material encapsulation of tensions between hierarchy and heterarchy, as well as the deep-time history of pluralistic institutions within the Southeastern United States.

Another relevant line of research on the built environment, based mostly in sociology, deals with public gathering spaces as "social infrastructure" that fosters more equitable and resilient communities by providing opportunities for neighbors to have face-to-face contact in recreational settings, such as libraries, parks, playing fields, and town squares (Klinenberg 2018). Scholars researching contemporary social infrastructure have found strong positive correlations between its equitable distribution and greater social capital in the form of more trusting and cooperative interpersonal relations within both urban and rural settings (Flora 1998; Latham and Layton 2019). In some cases, social infrastructure is a form of public good distributed by more collective civic or governmental agencies, while in others it can be instigated through self-organizing processes by more localized, community-driven configurations, such as by coordinated families or neighborhoods. In either case, its presence as an arena for convivial social interaction enables virtuous cycles of prosocial behavior (Blanton and Fargher 2011). As an example, US post offices in the nineteenth century could be considered somewhere between hard and social infrastructure, as they were gathering places that kept communities connected and information flowing between them. A historical survey of where they were

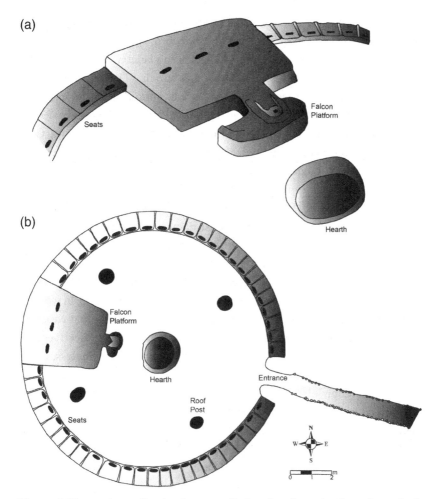

**Figure 3** Illustrations of a circular council chamber from the Ocmulgee site in Georgia, showing (a) reconstruction of falcon platform, adjacent seats, and central hearth (based on Dickens and McKinley [2003]) and (b) plan view illustration from excavations (based on Fairbanks [1946: fig. 21]).

first established and how many existed per county demonstrates strong correlations between the establishment of early post offices and higher incidences of social capital today, measured in indices such as having more per capita community newspapers and civic and social organizations, and fewer social ills, such as lower arrests and mortality rates (Jensen and Ramey 2020). Historical analyses of this type indicate that early investments in community infrastructure have long-term ramifications for social capital and community resilience (see also Putnam et al. 1993; Yue et al. 2022).

Issues of equity and social capital can also be evaluated through smaller-scale material remains in the archaeological record, such as distributions of artifacts and ecofacts, health indices reflected in skeletal remains, and the relative size and elaboration of houses and burials. These are all long-standing archaeological concerns, but recent approaches interested in understanding variability in past sociopolitical organization have found novel ways to evaluate them more empirically through calculating Gini indices using various archaeological proxies of wealth (e.g., Kohler and Smith 2018) or through comparative analyses of the fiscal financing of governance and institutional economies (Blanton and Fargher 2008: 112–132; Hirth 2020: 154–193). Much of the work on Gini calculations for gauging relative levels of inequality use domestic living space as a proxy, since it is widely generalizable to different cultural contexts unlike determining what commodities were valued in any setting or accounting for cultural variability in mortuary practices and furnishings. The most exclusive and inequitable architectural complexes of the premodern world were of course palaces, and any society centered on them or showing great variance between the sizes of elite and non-elite houses is clearly less collective than one in which living space was more equitably allocated. Nevertheless, other variables such as location, quality of construction materials, and elaborateness of decoration also figure prominently in the social differentiation materialized in houses (Blanton 1994).

Other archaeological signatures of fiscal systems and inequality include whether revenue streams for political economies were based more on staple or wealth goods (e.g., D'Altroy and Earle 1985) and the possibility for more exclusionary control along the lines illustrated in Figure 2. A few key axes of variability in how we interpret the collectivity of social organization as seen in the archaeological record are outlined in Table 1. Variables are generalized so that they could be applied to settings throughout the globe and also may be manifested in different types of material remains, necessitating integrated and multiscale analyses of space, things, and imagery. Most societies feature mixtures of attributes along these axes, and we need to envision possibilities of change over time, as gumlao/gumsa cycles or other well-documented societal oscillations highlight. We agree with Blanton and Fargher (2008: 293) that "Collective action process may be expressed in diverse cultural settings and time periods, and is especially sensitive to local conditions that have an impact on revenue streams, while cultural code may be a less influential causal force, or may be more of a dependent variable."

**Table 1** Axes of variability in more and less collective social organization.

| More Collective | Less Collective |
| --- | --- |
| Internal revenues: regularized taxation, a focus on staple finance and regional goods | External revenues: long-distance trade, importance of portable wealth, spoils of war, control of spot resources |
| More communally owned or managed land | Less communally owned or managed land |
| Fewer disparities of wealth in life and death | Greater disparities of wealth in life and death |
| Greater potential for shared power | Greater potential for individualized power |
| Political ideology emphasizes abstract principles of offices and strength of the polity, cosmology, and fertility | Political ideology emphasizes lineal descent systems for succession and legitimation, divine kingship and royal patron deities |
| Not centered on palaces | Centrality of palaces |
| Monumental architecture fosters access (e.g., open plazas, wide access-ways, community temples) | Monumental architecture fosters exclusivity (e.g., elite tombs and memorials, dynastic temples) |
| Greater expenditure on public goods | Smaller expenditure on public goods |

## 1.4 Summary

To this point, we have outlined a framework, drawn from a range of disciplines, that is focused on the contingent factors that foster or impede human cooperation and underpin diverse forms of collective action among social groups. Human agency, hence the potential for selfishness, is universal (Melis and Semmann 2010; Sökefeld 1999), and yet as a species we are unrivaled in our abilities to cooperate in large aggregations and affiliations with nonkin. For us, the key assignment is to outline the factors that constrain and foster such collaborative formations. Whereas scholars studying resource management, such as Ostrom (1990, 2005), tend to engage more with the allocation and organization of public goods among smaller groups of "conditional cooperators," those drawing on comparative historical cases, such as Levi (1988, 1996), take a more macro-approach to political and economic systems, and especially the role of revenue streams and fiscal financing. It is important to note that we do not see these approaches as at odds with one another; rather, they provide insights for dealing with different scales of human interaction.

In subsequent sections, we focus our conceptual lens on Mesoamerica, one of the parts of the world where a diversity of keystone institutions, urban settlements, large-scale polities, and extensive socioeconomic networks arose independently. Yet those interpersonal affiliations took a diversity of forms, across space and social scale, and they also varied markedly in cultural regions and through time. Although we recognize that our current interpretations and hypotheses are certainly not final, we hope that the new framing offered here provides a firmer foundation to understand the prehispanic Mesoamerican world and to integrate more comprehensively the lessons and Indigenous knowledge of that world into global comparisons and constructs.

## 2 Mesoamerica as a Region and Assemblage of Cultural Institutions

Mesoamerica is one of the most biodiverse parts of the globe, in terms of both flora and fauna, due to its varied ecology set within tropical latitudes featuring large mountain ranges and close proximity to the coastal storm systems of the Pacific to the west and the Gulf of Mexico/Caribbean/Atlantic to the east (Figure 4). Today it comprises approximately the southern two-thirds of Mexico, all of Guatemala and Belize, and parts of adjacent Central American countries. There are no clear natural boundaries to Mesoamerica as one heads

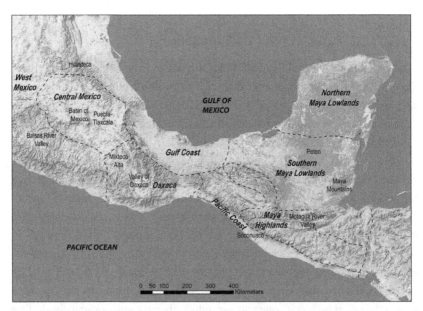

**Figure 4** Map of Mesoamerica depicting macroregions, such as central Mexico and the Maya lowlands, and selected regions discussed in the text.

south, while other sides of the culture area are circumscribed by seas or somewhat by the Chihuahuan and Sonoran Deserts to the north, a region that the Aztecs referred to as the Chichimeca. These boundaries are nevertheless porous and changed through time, with the result that Mesoamerica has always been defined through the shared cultural practices and institutions of interacting peoples rather than by geography.

The ecological diversity of Mesoamerica is matched by its ethnic and linguistic diversity, with Uto-Aztecan, Mayan, and Otomanguean representing the three largest language families (Kaufman and Justeson 2009). Most of the cases we will be discussing involve peoples of these language families, such as the Aztecs, Toltecs, and perhaps Teotihuacanos for the first, the Maya for the second, and the Mixtec and Zapotec for the third. Yet it is important to emphasize that these ethnonyms are relatively recent, arising from processes of European colonialism, and prehispanic Mesoamericans did not refer to themselves using these terms (Lockhart 1992; Restall and Gabbert 2017). Instead, precolonial peoples had strong sentiments of micro-patriotism to city-states or confederated polities. Indigenous peoples of Mesoamerica today more often use terms such as Nahuas, descendants of Aztec groups; Yucatec Maya or K'iche Maya, for two large ethnic groups within the Mayan language families; or the Be'ena'a for the Zapotec who, like many others, were bestowed with a Nahuatl name as the former Mexica-Aztec capital of Mexico-Tenochtitlan became the new colonial power center of New Spain. In this section, we will examine the well-documented cultural institutions of Mesoamerica with a particular emphasis on labor and resource management, governance, and other means of collective action.

## 2.1 Cultural Institutions and Social Theories

During the early twentieth century, anthropology and archaeology emphasized culture-history as researchers sought to define culture areas and create chronological sequences of their developments and associated material culture. The German-Mexican anthropologist Paul Kirchhoff (1943) first defined Mesoamerica along a series of traits that he compared with those of other peoples of the Americas. Subsequent research has shown how some of these traits are problematic while others are of uneven utility for studying the archaeological record, due mostly to differential preservation of organic remains and nonmaterial forms of culture (Creamer 1987). Among those traits or practices that Kirchhoff proposed as distinctive to Mesoamerica were a dual-calendar system combining the 365-day solar year with a 260-day ritual year; the processing of maize in an alkaline solution (nixtamalization), allowing for the formation of tortillas as a more nutritious staple food; specialized commercial markets; lakeshore wetland agricultural fields (*chinampas*); stepped temples covered in lime stucco; and ballcourts featuring rings for scoring. Of these, probably only the first three were present in most or all of Mesoamerica, but they are worth emphasizing as broadly shared means of coordinating people by parsing time and subsistence/ economic activities potentially amenable to collective action. Team sports such as Mesoamerican ballgames provide a nice encapsulation of human dynamics of cooperation with an in-group in order to compete with an out-group, and whether or not temples represent a public good depends on how they are used and what symbolic messaging they convey, as we saw in Section 1. In a next tier of traits present in Mesoamerica but also in other parts of the Americas, Kirchhoff listed agricultural terraces, specialized craft economies, and the importance of intermediate-scale corporate-kin groups such as the Aztec *calpolli* ("big house") – all also relevant to considerations of how people affiliated with nonkin and worked either cooperatively or antagonistically.

More recently, Mesoamerican scholars have considered the culture area as an assemblage of institutions, rather than checkbox-type trait lists as were compiled by cultural historians, allowing for more comparative assessment by subregions or through time. Pervasive keystone institutions at the time of the Spanish invasion included in domains we could categorize as politics (states); settlement tiers (cities, neighborhoods/barrios, rural communities, households); economics (marketplaces and irrigation societies); and ritual/religion (temples) (Kowalewski and Heredia 2020). A reframing of the Mesoamerican past to emphasize institutions and individual practices within them (see Joyce 2021) allows us to query issues such as the relationship between social scale or population with the number of institutions, their complexity, or their degrees of collectivity and trust, and to identify which institutions contributed to sustaining or worked to undermine collective action.

Relationships between the scale of societies and the nature of their institutions turn out to be not as tightly correlated or predictable as early models of social evolution imagined. For instance, rather than observing clear correlations between social scale and the likelihood that resource systems will be successfully self-organized, comparative analyses by Ostrom (2005: 251–252) and others highlight the greater importance of actors making strategic tradeoffs between the costs of providing a public good or managing a common-pool resource (for instance, in transaction costs or in sanctioning for noncompliance) and overall value of the resource system (for instance, the subtractability of the particular resource). Operating at the highest level of concentrated power and largest scale of polities, Levi (1996: 10–16) emphasizes the critical role of trust in state institutions to societal stability and the historical resilience of governing systems that (1) make credible commitments to its citizens, (2) are seen by them as upholding fair procedures, and (3) foster reciprocal sentiments of trust. She also identified key factors affecting perceptions of fairness as involving a combination of (a) coercion or sanctioning of those who neglect their responsibilities, (b) cultivation of a universalistic, merit-based ethos, (c) creation of impartial institutions (judicial, electoral), and (d) more pluralistic decision-making allowing for broad participation in the institutions of governance (see also Levi 2022). Several of Levi's points overlap with efforts by archaeologists to define corporate cognitive codes that have historically promoted more pluralistic systems of governance (e.g., Fargher 2016). It is worth considering both sets of relationships in the light of Mesoamerican institutions for managing resources and governing.

A reframing of Mesoamerican archaeology around institutions, including some of the ethnographic traits used in cultural-historical definitions like Kirchhoff's, enables more multiscalar, comparative analyses and moves us beyond top-down or unilinear evolutionary models of societal development. Top-down perspectives of Mesoamerican sociopolitical organization derive primarily from two historical currents of the twentieth century: an early sample bias in archaeological research towards seats of power – political capitals, their temples and palaces – and elite material culture such as tombs and courtly art; and the uncritical use of ideas stemming from Marxist historical materialism, corresponding to modes of production as stages of evolution to group early cultures, such as "Oriental Despotism" (Blanton and Fargher 2016: 99–106; Gándara 2012; Offner 1981). While the mid-twentieth-century shift to consider settlements across the entire scalar spectrum and the houses of non-elites helped to start to rectify the top-down biases of archaeologists excavating only pyramids and palaces, conclusions of the research were also often framed using unilinear models of societal development that did not allow for variable forms of organization and institutions. Our goal in this section is to illustrate precisely that variability.

## 2.2 Indigenous Mesoamerican Institutions of Working Together

> The work of the youths and maidens was communal labor [coatequitl]. They made bundles of wood for the houses of the rulers and there in Mexico they made bundles of wood and they fixed up the roads as well as wherever stone enclosures were built and wherever mist houses [water sanctuaries] were located. The real work of the youths and maidens was that they sang and danced holding hands. (Sahagún 1997: chapter III, paragraph 13, p. 221)

A rotary tax delivered in labor, sometimes referred to using the French term *corveé* and also as labor tribute, was a key institution of Aztec society and is documented among other Mesoamerican groups as well (Carballo 2013b; Rojas Rabiela 1977, 1986). The above passage was written by Nahua scribes working in a trilingual (Nahuatl, Spanish, and Latin) documentation project

overseen by the Spanish friar Bernardino de Sahagún in the decades following the establishment of colonial New Spain. It speaks to a type of civic
service termed *coatequitl* – literally "snake/twin work" but implying a sense
of reciprocity – performed by youths on behalf of their ethnic state (the
*altepetl*) as part of their compulsory system of education open to all youths
(the *telpochcalli*) and covering subjects we might gloss as civics, history,
calendrics, martial arts, religion, and ritual. The rich historical corpus from
sixteenth-century central Mexico, compiled by both Spanish and Indigenous
authors, makes such institutions of the greater Aztec world the best known
for Mesoamerica. In Table 2, we provide some examples of Nahuatl terms
relating to key resources and the social and political institutions involved in
managing them. Some terms overlap and represent regional variability, but
they help us move from abstract notions of collective action by providing
concrete examples of Indigenous institutions and potential axes of variability
within them. We also consider parallel cases among other Mesoamerican
peoples.

Forms of collective labor that mirror the Nahuatl terms *tequitl* –
a suprahousehold scale yet smaller than town or polity – and coatequitl are
still practiced by descendant Indigenous and mestizo (mixed, Spanish-
speaking) communities in Mesoamerica today. They are well-documented
ethnographically through the twentieth century, including in Nahua communities of central Mexico (Good 2005; Lewis 1963: 108–111), Maya communities of the Yucatan (Redfield and Villa Rojas 1967: 77–80), and Mixtec
(Monaghan 1990) and Zapotec (Cohen 1999) communities of Oaxaca. Labor
is typically organized through social units intermediate in scale between
households and towns or municipalities. Depending on the setting, the
intermediating units might be Spanish synonyms for neighborhoods, such
as *barrios* or *colonias*, or may be termed *demarcaciones* or *secciones*,
usually implying something larger along the lines of a ward or district.
Work teams tackle public infrastructure projects involving water systems,
roads, churches and municipal buildings, schools, and social infrastructure
such as recreational fields. Some examples of contemporary, small-scale
water acquisition and distribution infrastructure from the semiarid highlands
of Oaxaca are illustrated in Figure 5 and include wells for tapping groundwater and check dams and irrigation channels for capturing rainfall and
distributing it to fields.

In communal work of this type, individuals who neglect their labor duties
might be sanctioned through fines or even jail time, while participants in the
system are rewarded through collective meals and the positive reputation that
comes with good citizenship – a form of ritual economy that Monaghan (1996)

**Table 2** Selected Nahuatl Terms Relating to Land, Infrastructure, Social Organization, and Governance.

| Term | Translation | Significance |
|------|-------------|-------------|
| Land | | |
| *altepetlalli* | "altepetl land" | land of a polity |
| *calpoltlalli* | "calpolli land" | land of a suprahousehold corporate group |
| *cihuatlalli* | "woman's land" | land held by a woman and perhaps used as dowry |
| *pillalli* | "noble's land" | land of a non-ruling noble |
| *tecpantlalli* | "tecpan land" | land associated with a palace |
| *teopantlalli* | "temple land" | land associated with a temple |
| *tequitlalli* | "tribute land" | land worked as part of labor tax/tribute |
| *teuctlalli* | "ruler's land" | land of a titled lord or ruler |
| *tlacohualli* | "purchased land" | land purchased commercially |
| Labor | | |
| *coatequitl* | "snake/twin work" | public (altepetl level) rotary labor tax/tribute |
| *tecpantlaca* | "palace people" | labor attached to a royal palace |
| *tequitl* | "work-tribute" | suprahousehold labor obligations |
| *tlacalaquilli* | "something delivered" | rotary tax obligations |
| Infrastructure | | |
| *aotli* | "water road" | aqueduct |
| *apantli* | "water walls" | irrigation canal |
| *calpolco* | "calpolli place" | neighborhood center, usually with temple |
| *calmecac* | "house of the lineage" | elite school |
| *otli* | "road" | path or road |
| *telpochcalli* | "house of youths" | non-elite school |
| *teocalli* | "god house" | temple |
| *tianquiztli* | "market" | open-air marketplace |
| *tlapantli* | "land wall" | agricultural terrace |
| Social Groups | | |
| *calpolli* | "big house" | suprahousehold corporate-kin group |
| *chinamitl* | "fenced-in field" | neighborhood (in chinampa zones, e.g., Chalco) |
| *teccalli* | "lord's house" | patrimonial noble estate |
| *tlaca* | "person" | neighborhood (in Tlaxcallan) |
| *tlaxilacalli* | "house pierced by water" | suprahousehold territorial unit, neighborhood |
| *tlayacatl* | "something governed" | division of a larger polity like a complex altepetl |

**Table 2** (cont.)

| Term | Translation | Significance |
|------|-------------|--------------|
| Governance | | |
| *altepetl* | "water mountain" | polity, realm, "city-state" (pl. *altepemeh*) |
| *calpixque* | "house guardian" | tax collector, tribute steward |
| *cihuacoatl* | "woman snake" | chief of internal administration |
| *pilli* | "children of nobles" | non-ruling nobles often in bureaucratic roles |
| *quauhpilli* | "eagle nobles" | commoner achieving quasi-nobility (e.g., via war) |
| *ququhtlatoni* | "eagle speaker" | ruler through achievement, typically interim |
| *tecuhtli/teuctli* | "lord" | titled head of a noble house with land & followers |
| *teuctlato(ni)* | "lord speaker" | judge, calpolli head |
| *tequitlato* | "work/tribute speaker" | (labor) tax collector, tribute steward |
| *tlaixquetzaliztli* | "election" | election of a person to office |
| *tlatoani* | "speaker" | ruler (pl. *tlatoque*; prefix *huey* = "great") |
| *tlatocan* | "place of speakers" | ruling council |
| *tlatocayotl* | "speaker father" | rulership in more established dynasties |

**Sources:** Alcántara Gallegos (2004); Berdan (2014:Table 6.1); Fargher et al. (2017, 2022); Hicks (1984); Hirth (2016:Table 2.1); Lockhart (1992); Molina (2008); Restall and Meyer (personal communication 2023); Reyes (2020); Rojas Rabiela (1977, 1986); Schroeder (1991); Smith (2015); Zorita (1963).

has alliteratively termed "fiesta finance." Group work responsibilities often represent one of the defining principles for Mesoamerican community affiliation (Cohen 1999: 9; Monaghan 1990: 768). In fact, in the central Mexican state of Tlaxcala during the mid-twentieth century public works were referred to as *comunidad* (community) and were an expected weekly contribution on the part of adult males. One project within a seasonal wetland environment (*humedal*) was documented by Wilken (1968: 228) as involving more than 100 community members who participated in maintaining the common-pool resource of a drained-field system by clearing and widening canals over two days, overseen and celebrated by municipal officials.

The example of drained-field maintenance in the wetlands of southern Tlaxcala evokes the most intensive agricultural systems of prehispanic Mesoamerica: the chinampas (*chinamitl*) constructed along the lakeshores of the Basin of Mexico (Cordova 2022: 196, 206–214; Frederick 2007). As a form

**Figure 5** Photos of water management infrastructure in the contemporary Valley of Oaxaca, including (a) a small well, (b) check dams, and (c) a small irrigation channel.

of landesque capital that involved sunk costs of labor to create and continually maintain, with the payoff of exceptionally productive agricultural yields, chinampas involved the interplay of institutions that could be classified as top-down and bottom-up (Morehart 2017, 2018). In the most productive setting of the southern freshwater lakes, Aztec chinampas had a long and narrow configuration, measuring approximately 50 m by less than 4 m, and as much as half of the crops grown on them were ceded to imperial tax officials as a tax in kind. Relic Aztec canals could still be seen in aerial photos of the 1940s (Luna Golya 2014), while fields that remained active at that time had been modified into shorter and wider parcels (Figure 6). Certain pre-Aztec chinampas of the saline northern lakes were, in contrast, abandoned following imperial expansion in the region. Like other resource systems, chinampa management therefore involved political dynamics between users and governing structures who, in this case, oversaw intensification efforts in order to provide a consistent, internal tax base in staple goods.

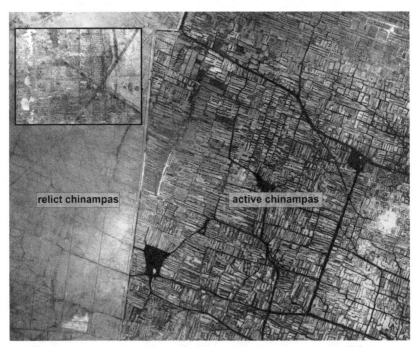

**Figure 6** Base image shows (left) relic Aztec chinampas and (right) active chinampas from a 1941 aerial photo modified from the Compañía Mexicana Aerofoto, while inset image shows the similar configuration of the chinampas from the sixteenth-century Plano Parcial de la Ciudad de México (Mediateca INAH). https://mediateca.inah.gob.mx/islandora_74/islandora/object/codice%3A635

Chinampas and other agricultural fields existed on land that was managed as a resource along a spectrum from private to common-pool, as indicated in Figure 2. The Nahuatl land terms in Table 2 provide an indication of land that was more privately owned, typically by nobles or other social elites, and land that was owned and managed by suprahousehold corporate groups. In the case of the latter, use was allocated to individual families, making them semi-privatized, but under norms of land tenure that fields would be tended to or risk being absorbed and reallocated by the calpolli or another corporate group (Harvey 1984; Hirth 2016: 36–41; Lockhart 1992: 141–163). The base of Aztec and other Mesoamerican subsistence economies thereby rested on land and the labor required to construct and maintain infrastructure of agricultural intensification, such as irrigation canals and terraces (Rojas Rabiela et al. 2009). These networks of subsistence infrastructure were generally managed as common-pool resources because, although individual fields may be allocated to particular families, any dereliction in maintaining one's individual segments of the system adversely impacted others. Communal lands such as those managed by a calpolli (*calpotlalli*) also included forest lands that included various common-pool resources that were in the group's interest not to overexploit, such as stocks of lumber and game (Harvey 1984: 91).

Critical to the organization of Aztec labor obligations was the coordination provided by the ceremonial calendar and its associated sequence of monthly (twenty-day) rites (Gillespie 1989: 210–215; van Zantwijk 1985: 24–25). The ceremonial calendar "mapped social relations in space and time" (Gillespie 1989: 211). This calendrical scheduling of communal labor is emphasized by the Nahua author of the quote at the beginning of this section, discussing coatequitl and then noting how the work of the youths and maidens involved singing and dancing while holding hands. As a result, the keeping of the ceremonial calendar by priests or others trained in calendrical and glyphic notation in elite religious schools (*calmecac*) constituted an important bureaucratic role for the organization of labor in Aztec society and likely also in other Mesoamerican societies that kept calendrical records through hieroglyphic notation or oral histories.

Famously lacking in the subsistence economies of Mesoamerica were large domesticated animals, an important point of contrast with other nuclear areas of early agriculture and urbanism in Afro-Eurasia and South America. This deficit had at least two important implications regarding social organization and resource management. The first is that large domesticated animals often drove increased inequality in early societies since, depending on the setting, they could represent "wealth on hoof" in and of themselves; they could be used for plowing fields and creating more extensive tracts of arable land; or they could be used in warfare or raiding (Boix 2015: 140–159; Glowacki 2020; Kohler et al. 2017). In all cases, large domesticates had the potential to create and exacerbate disparities in wealth and power that were not available pathways to these ends for aspiring Mesoamerican elites. The second implication is that the management of hunted game species, fisheries, and concentrations of collected resources remained more important among Mesoamerican societies than was the case for many other early agriculturalists. Along these lines, Jeffrey Parsons (2008), who spent decades studying the collecting of aquatic resources in the Basin of Mexico and the use of drought-tolerant plants, like cacti and succulents, proposed that these activities provided functional and nutritional equivalents of pastoral niches in Mesoamerica. The cultivation and processing of maguey and other agaves found in more arid regions fostered suprahousehold management and gender complementarity in labor (Evans 2005). Fishing, hunting waterfowl, salt production, and the collection of lacustrine resources such as insects and algae did not require large groups, but they created communities with shared identities, networks, and patron deities and offered "opportunities for cooperation, possibilities for conflict, ecological change, and other unintended consequences" (Millhauser 2017: 311). In other words, these functional equivalents of pastoralism in Mesoamerica were structured by different dynamics of resource management than true pastoralism, creating more common-pool resource issues than are typical for privately owned herds of animals.

In addition to studies of subsistence economies, recent research on Aztec markets and exchange systems helps to distinguish what fiscal streams were more internal to a particular polity, what were more external or mixed strategies, and how these revenue streams were allocated to supporting a bureaucratic infrastructure and dissemination of public goods to varying degrees (Blanton and Fargher 2012; Hirth 2016; Nichols et al. 2017). Central Mexican economies were commercialized prior to the Aztec empire, and the strategies of Tenochtitlan and Texcoco in particular focused generally on encouraging pre-existing market systems and trade networks, or incentivizing the creation of new ones, though they also intervened militarily in punitive ways in cases of political dissent from provincial centers. Exotic items originating outside of central Mexico and luxury items requiring skilled labor in their manufacture made their way disproportionately to Aztec elites through systems of imperial tribute and palace-based coatequitl, and certain forms of dress and adornment were restricted to nobility based on sumptuary laws, but a range of jewelry and other luxury items were also available in marketplaces for individuals who had the purchasing power to obtain them (Hirth 2016: 52–57, table 3.1). This could include a "middle class" in Aztec society of non-nobles with achieved status through service in the military or in the political bureaucracy, skilled artisanship or long-distance trade, and as priests or other ritual specialists (Hicks 1999). More widely available were "bulk luxuries" such as highly decorative polychrome pottery, made within central Mexico but requiring skilled manufacture, and valued commodities from outside of central Mexico, including cacao and cotton. These became more widely available to non-elites in the Late Postclassic than they had been during earlier periods of Mesoamerican history (Blanton et al. 2005) and moved through complex commodity chains that saw fluid and overlapping relationships between intermediate or "mesoscale" social groups amendable to analysis using collective action frameworks (Millhauser and Overhaltzer 2020).

Aztec tax systems in goods and labor, and questions relating to the financing of states and other political institutions, bring us to the issue of governance and its variable organization documented among cases from the Aztec world and other parts of Postclassic Mesoamerica.

## 2.3 Indigenous Institutions of Mesoamerican Governance

> To your government, to your lordship, you bring honor, you make it prosper, and that is because you work intensely for it … A long time ago the lords, the governors, came to lay the foundation, came to establish the principle of rule, of governance … In all parts they smoothed, polished, did good, brought order, with prudence, with happiness, with tranquility … Perhaps the lords, the governors, also bestowed upon you the leadership, the channeling, that which educates people, that which instructs … Do not carry your burden with laziness; do not neglect, do not turn your back on your water, your mountain [*altepetl* or polity]; do it good.
>
> (León-Portilla 1991: 380–395; translation by authors)

We are able to glean prehispanic Mesoamerican perspectives on what constituted good governance from passages such as the one above, which is a compilation of *huehuehtlahtolli* ("words of the ancients") recorded by the friar Andrés de Olmos working with Nahuatl-speaking scribes in the 1530s, a little over a decade removed from the Spanish-Aztec War. When people use the term Aztec colloquially, they are often referring to the Mexica ethnic group and, more specifically, the Tenochca-Mexica who occupied the imperial capital of Tenochtitlan. This problematic shorthand muddles understanding because a broader definition of Aztec – for instance, the peoples of Postclassic central Mexico with a shared narrative of origins in Aztlan – includes tremendous diversity in forms of governance, equal to or greater than what existed in Europe at the time (Carballo 2022) (Figure 7). Alonso de Zorita (1963: 86), the sixteenth-century Spanish chronicler who recorded a wealth of information on land, labor, and governance in prehispanic Mexico noted, "it is impossible to state a general rule as concerns any part of Indian Government and customs, for there are great differences in almost every province." The micro-patriotism and

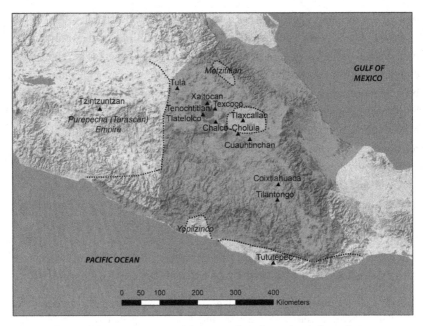

**Figure 7** Map of western Mesoamerica, featuring selected sites
and areas of political hegemony by Aztec (Triple Alliance) empire
(shaded) and rival states (dotted lines). https://mediateca.inah.gob.mx/islan
dora_74/islandora/object/codice%3A635

divergent views of governance within the Aztec world are nicely illustrated by
a passage in book 12 of the *Florentine Codex*, where a scribe from the Mexica
sister-city of Tlatelolco, occupying the same island as Tenochtitlan, evinces his
low regard for Moctezuma II (or Xocoyotzin), the tlatoani of Tenochtitlan,
compared with Itzquauhtzin, the tlatoani of Tlatelolco. In funeral services for
both rulers during the Spanish-Aztec War, we are told that people cursed
Moctezuma's name, as he had been feared, and when his funeral pyre was lit
the ruler's body gave off a foul stench; Itzquauhtzin, in contrast, was grieved,
wept for, and cremated with great splendor (Lockhart 1993: 150–152).

   Also emphasized by Nahua scribes in recording the oral histories of the elders
is the centrality of the altepetl to political organization and a moral philosophy
of rulership legitimated on the basis of historical precedent set by past governors
said to have ruled justly and prudently. Although the term altepetl is often
glossed in English as city-state, the metaphoric couplet of waters and mountains
evokes a territorial realm or polity with the urban component of secondary
importance. Historical records document a diverse array of altepetl organization, ranging from polities with a single ruler (Tenochtitlan) to others with as
many as seven corulers (Cuauhtinchan) (Lockhart 1992: 14–58; Paulinyi 1981).

Confederated polities, such as Chalco and Tlaxcallan, were also a common arrangement and could have four or more corulers plus large and powerful governing councils featuring more pluralistic institutions of decision-making (Gutiérrez Mendoza 2012).

Even Tenochtitlan, the most powerful city in prehispanic Mesoamerican history, was part of a confederation between three altepemeh. Its paramount ruler, the "great speaker" (*huey tlatoni*), ruled in consultation with the rulers of those polities along with another powerful Tenochca (the *cihuacoatl* or "woman snake") and a council of four dignitaries (Pastrana Flores 2020: 123–126). Later Tenochca rulers appear to have purposefully suppressed an earlier history of quadripartite corule beginning with the empire builder Itzcoatl (r. 1427–1440), who ordered earlier histories be destroyed to recast rulership in more autocratic terms, a centralization of power that culminated under Moctezuma II (Hassig 2016: 56; Lockhart 1992: 25; López Austin 1961: 20–52). Other documents reveal that for some fifty years following its founding Tenochtitlan had no single ruler and, as a subject polity to Colhuacan and then Azcapotzalco, was governed internally by the tlatoani of its barrios or wards (Moyotlan, Teopan, Atzacualco, and Cuepopan), who retained autonomous authority to organize calpollis to build and maintain infrastructure through the city's transition to an imperial capital (Figure 8) (Florescano 2017: 100; Hassig 2016: 26). As a multiethnic capital, Tenochtitlan's political organization was deliberately divided into factions with different, complementary roles in the system:

> These interethnic institutions were, in fact, mechanisms that maintained the balance of power in a government that could easily disintegrate if high-level cooperation was disrupted. The indigenous Mexican empire builders reduced the risk of such a split by making their interethnic systems of government mutually complementary. That is to say, they divided government operations among the various ethnic groups in such a way that the state could function only through their cooperation. Each group was responsible for only a part of the system; therefore, no segment could independently regulate it. (van Zantwijk 1985: 25)

Direct succession of rulership from parent to child, whether following primogeniture or not, was the exception rather than the rule in the Aztec world, with the imperial "second city" of Texcoco representing one of the notable exceptions (Carrasco 1984; Offner 2010). Succession was more typically collateral, meaning it was determined through election by ruling councils from a slate of candidates from certain noble families, and represented a more fluid system than was practiced by the Postclassic period Mixtec and Classic period Maya (Carrasco 1984: 46; Hassig 2016: 30–59; Marcus 1992: 306–320; van Zantwijk 1985: 25, 178–179). During the Postclassic period, succession within Mixtec kingdoms most closely adhered to rules of primogeniture and a concern with maintaining

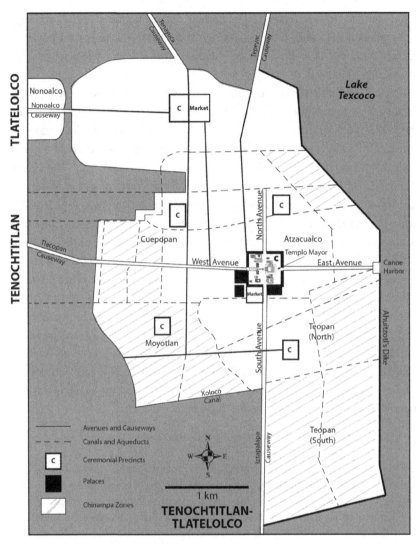

**Figure 8** Map reconstructing Tenochtitlan-Tlatelolco in the sixteenth century, with depictions of Tenochtitlan's four wards or barrios, ceremonial precincts, chinampa zones, and other features of urban infrastructure.

royal bloodlines, which were legitimated materially through art emphasizing royal genealogy (Figure 9), the focal role of palaces within urban centers, and what were perhaps the most elaborate tombs and personal ornamentation from prehispanic Mesoamerica (Caso 1966; Spores and Balkansky 2013: 89–103). Mixtec codices foreground royal genealogies and the exploits of certain kings and queens yet also indicate the presence of small councils that served political and

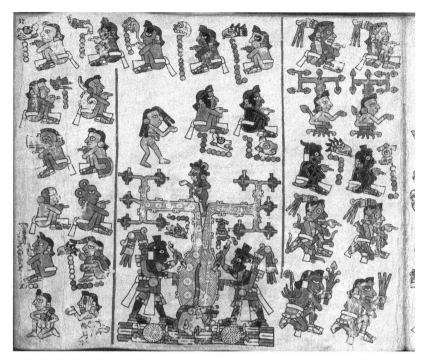

**Figure 9** Scene from prehispanic Mixtec codex (Codex Vindobonensis) depicting noble genealogy and founding narrative of emergence from sacred tree. Austrian National Library, Vienna.

religious functions (Jansen and Pérez Jiménez 2011: 357–461; Pohl 1994). Aztec and other central Mexican codices, in turn, more frequently depict cosmological themes relating to the ritual calendar (critical to coordinating communal labor), migration narratives of ethnogenesis, and tax records, though individual rulers were depicted in postconquest codices and in a few instances of prehispanic sculpture, particularly under the more consolidated rule of Moctezuma II (Hajovsky 2015).

Although the Mixtec kingdoms were in close contact with the peoples of Tlaxcallan, current Tlaxcala, these major rivals to the Mexica-Aztec developed a very different system of governance, likely in a process analogous to schismogenesis as a form of resistance to the imperial ambitions of the Triple Alliance. Tlaxcallan's governance structure was highly pluralistic, with Cortés (1986: 68) equating it to the northern Italian republics he knew from Europe. Tlaxcaltec political organization featured a distribution of executive power through rotating officeholders, a governing council that probably numbered in the hundreds of members and included some level of participation on

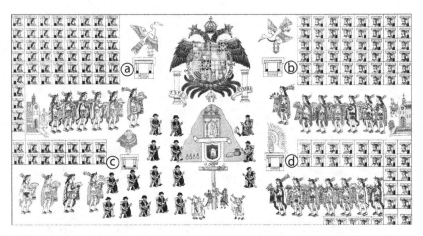

**Figure 10** Scene from colonial period Lienzo de Tlaxcala, depicting ruling figures and houses represented in the council governance of (a) Tizatlan, (b) Ocotolulco, (c) Tepeticpac, and (d) Quiahuiztlan.

the part of non-elites, and no clear cases of residences that could have served as central palaces (Fargher et al. 2010, 2011, 2022; López Corral 2023). Aspirants to high office, the *teuhctli*, underwent elaborate ceremonies of investiture involving acts of penance, self-sacrifice, and fasting that could last up to a year (Reyes 2020). During the early colonial period, the Tlaxcaltecs presented themselves to the Spanish Crown as a confederation of four nearby city-states: Tizatlan, Ocotolulco, Tepeticpac, and Quiahuiztlan (Figure 10). Although conquistadors singled out Xicotencatl the elder and Maxixcatzin, representing the first two of these divisions, leading figures of other important factions in the governance structure are also named and the four-part confederation seems a colonial period reconfiguration of what were previously wards or districts of a single urban agglomeration (Lockhart 1992: 20–23). The city was organized as a polycentric yet interconnected network of residential terraces and equitably distributed social infrastructure of plazas, small shrines, and altars, with a disembedded ritual precinct not connected to any one faction (Fargher et al. 2011, 2022). Governance in Tlaxcallan can be said to have featured democratic institutions and was also inclusive in terms of the definition of citizenship, with ethnic groups other than the dominant Nahuas, such as the Otomi and Pinome, afforded that status (Fargher et al. 2022: 124).

To the south of Tlaxcallan, Cholula (former Chololan), was one of the most prominent market and pilgrimage centers of Postclassic Mesoamerica. Its inhabitants turned from being allies of the Tlaxcaltecs to becoming largely foes once Cholula was incorporated into the Triple Alliance empire.

**Figure 11** Depiction of the city of Cholula from the *Historia Tolteca Chichimeca* with temple to Quetzalcoatl at center left, calmecac at lower right, calpoltin in rectangles along border, and rulership structure with the corulers (a) Tlachiach and (b) Aquiach, ruler of internal affairs the (c) Chichimecatl teuctli, and (d) noble council in the "turquoise house." Base images from Wikimedia (https://commons.wikimedia.org/) and Bibliothèque nationale de France.

Documentary evidence indicates that Cholula's leadership structure was somewhere between Tlaxcallan and Tenochtitlan in terms of its pluralism as it featured two high priests who coruled the polity and were charged with external affairs, the *Tlachiach* and *Aquiach*, another ruler charged with internal affairs, the *Chichimecatl teuctli*, and a noble council depicted in the map of the city in the *Historia Tolteca Chichimeca* (Figure 11) as the "turquoise house" (Lind 2012; López Corral 2023; Plunket and Uruñuela 2018). The six councillors of the turquoise house acted as legislators and judges and were responsible for electing the three rulers in consultation with a larger governing council. Cholula's more oligarchic governance, relative to Tlaxcallan, is apparent in the fact that the *Tlachiach* and *Aquiach* could only be selected from among the nobility of a single, highly ranked calpolli (Carrasco 1971: 372).

The complex altepetl of Chalco was detailed by the prolific Nahua chronicler Chimalpahin and its political organization had several points of overlap with Tlaxcallan's, though its four altepemeh were more geographically dispersed and the polity's rules of succession and governing council were more restrictive. Chimalpahin's chronicles list some thirteen royal titles for the four altepemeh, each of which oversaw four to six suprahousehold groups, designated as calpolli, chinamitl, tlaxilacalli, and other terms listed in Table 2 and discussed in subsequent sections (Schroeder 1991: 109–113). In succession patterns, Chalco's governance structure might have been more dynastic or lineage based, akin to Mixtec polities, yet the "Chalca reveal considerably more flexibility, allowing the succession of commoners, the exchange of rulerships, and atypical marriage arrangements" (Schroeder 1991: 220). Interestingly, both the Chalca and the Mixtec featured more queens as paramount rulers than did more elective or pluralistic systems since maintenance of lineage ties was of greater concern and male-dominated councils tended to elect other men as successors to high office, a tendency seen in the kingdoms of early modern Iberia as well (Carballo 2020: 116).

Through this selected set of cases from the Postclassic period, we can appreciate some of the temporal changes in political organization and governance, such as is documented for Tenochtitlan, and the regional variability in the same observed between more dynastically oriented Mixtec kingdoms and more pluralistic Tlaxcallan, or elsewhere in Mesoamerica as well. A notable example from the Maya world is the operation of corule or council rule (*multepal*) at Mayapan and possibly other Postclassic capitals of the northern Yucatan (Masson and Peraza Lope 2014). The diversity of sociopolitical arrangements underscores the need to consider the same fluidity in earlier periods, which we will do in Section 3. Nevertheless, much of the literature on prehispanic Mesoamerican politics fixates on rulers and carries implicit assumptions of top-down leadership structures, while our aim is to consider political relations and governance more broadly so as to include multiple levels of interaction on the part of various social groups, bureaucratic roles, and the public goods and expectations placed on leaders in different polities. Some terms in Nahuatl that provide actual Mesoamerican examples appear in the infrastructure and governance sections of Table 2, while Figure 12 provides a schematic model for considering governance and collective action within Aztec polities. The model proposes that societies with more internal resource bases as fiscal streams are positively correlated with greater bureaucratization and dissemination of public goods (Blanton and Fargher 2008: 250–254) as members of state bureaucracies assume roles both in mobilizing internal resources via tax regimes and in organizing public labor. These variables also are positively correlated with checks on governing authorities, who relinquish elements of their decision-making in a bargain with subjects to, following Levi (1996: 10–16), (1) make credible commitments, implicating public goods; (2) uphold generally agreed

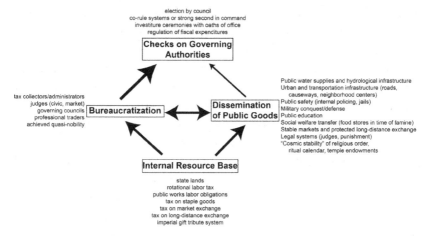

**Figure 12** Schematic text-and-arrow model of collective action with examples of public goods, internal revenues financing government, and types of accountability of leaders provided from Aztec states drawing on Blanton and Fargher (2008: 251–254) and sources cited in Table 2.

Arrow width reflects correlation strength between the variables in the authors' sample of thirty societies including Aztec but is calibrated for all cases.

upon fair procedures, through bureaucratic roles and checks on rulers; and (3) foster reciprocal sentiments of trust that sustain the general compliance of taxpayers who finance the system. The text adjacent to these key variables to collective action provides examples from the Aztec world, many of which have analogs for other culture regions and time periods in Mesoamerica.

In Blanton and Fargher's (2008) comparative study of thirty premodern states, the Aztec empire scored as tied with the Mughal empire as the sixth most collective and as in the top quarter of cases in terms of its dissemination of public goods, degree of bureaucratization, and checks on authorities. Yet, as we saw in the comparative cases discussed earlier, the Tenochca-Mexica were by no means the most pluralistic governance system of Postclassic Mesoamerica and its rulers had increasingly consolidated power during the imperial period, particularly under Moctezuma II. Based on textual accounts of the governance structure, Tlaxcallan was much more pluralistic, but it is useful to engage archaeological evidence pertaining to the built environment and relative levels of access to resources on the part of a broader populace. For instance, a comparison of Gini coefficients calculated based on the amount of residential living area scores Tenochtitlan (0.30) higher than Tlaxcallan (0.23) as we would expect, though both are considerably lower than the contemporary United States (0.49) and many premodern Eurasian state capitals (Fargher et al. 2022; Kohler et al. 2017). How much a differential economic base, lacking in large domesticated animals, utilitarian metals, and with fewer opportunities for elites to monopolize spot resources, relates to these values of more equitable living space is an important question that requires further study.

Although later Tenochca-Mexica rulers lived in large and lavish palaces, depicted themselves in state art on equal footing with gods, and conveyed their hegemony through ceremonies involving human sacrifice, they also had limits on their power and were expected to distribute public goods in the form of providing food stores in times of famine, constructing hydraulic projects such as aqueducts to bring fresh water in and dikes to keep flooding at bay, and expand the city's agricultural base through major canal systems that could take several years to construct (Berdan 2014: 76–81; Rojas Rabiela et al. 2009). A nice encapsulation of this comes from Chapultepec, located on the mainland to the west of Tenochtitlan. Here, Mexica sovereigns had their pleasure palaces and gardens but also oversaw projects to channel the hill's freshwater springs into the city via aqueducts – a pattern continuing into the viceroyalty of New Spain and representing a semipublic colonial park almost a century earlier than Boston Common (Cervantes de Salazar 1554/2014: 131). By bureaucratizing economic roles associated with markets and trade networks, the Mexica political economy also fostered broad sentiments of fairness in exchange by establishing principles of judicial neutrality in marketplaces such as Tlatelolco and in the entrepreneurial agency permitted to the *pochteca* and other merchant and artisan groups (Blanton and Fargher 2016: 96). State judicial and military oversight of fair and free trade were therefore public goods but paid for by taxes in kind and on markets and labor, which included military conscription. Irrespective of how Aztec rulers were promoting themselves, then, Aztec governance falls on the more collective or pluralistic end of the spectrum when we consider broader relationships between economic systems, bureaucracies, and public goods. Governance that we identify as more autocratic, in contrast, tends to be transactional to revolve around exclusionary networks of political or social elites.

A key axis of variability well documented in Aztec institutions underlay the tensions between forms of social organization based on hierarchical class relations, between nobles and commoners or patrons and clients, and among corporate groups with greater rank or status parity internally and heterarchical relations externally. In Nahuatl terminology, the tension was foremost between hierarchical patrimonial noble estates (the teccalli) and heterarchical corporate groups connected by kin and affinal ties (the calpolli and tlaxilacalli) or by economic bonds arising from shared occupation and market interests (the pochteca and certain high-status artisan groups). These institutions can likely be generalized to other Mesoamerican states, though we must be cautions as terms were used differently even within Postclassic central Mexico, with notable distinctions in terms between eastern and western Nahuas. For instance, subdivisions of the altepetl in eastern Nahua polities such as Tlaxcallan and Cuauhtinchan were often termed teccalli, while in western Nahua polities such as Chalco they were often termed tlayacatl, though particularly in the case of Tlaxcallan the teccalli subdivision was much less hierarchical than how the term was used to the west and allowed for achieved noble status (Fargher et al. 2022; Schroeder 1991: 215–216). Further, in some cases the standard of living for a non-elite may have been higher as a subject to an affluent noble in a teccalli structure than as a more autonomous member of a calpolli that possessed little land or social status. Still, Lockhart (1992: 98) rightfully emphasized the teccalli–calpolli tension as critical for understanding variability in precolonial Nahua sociopolitical organization, noting: "Teccalli and calpolli competed, threatening in principle to swallow each other up . . . Where the noble and patrimonial teccalli won out, the majority of the population might be special dependents . . . where the ethnic calpolli was predominant, the majority would be ordinary macehualtin [commoners]." A generalized notion of these two institutions from the Aztec world, including their fuzzy boundaries and tensions as hierarchical versus heterarchical bonds of affiliation, provides Indigenous templates grounded in historical texts for evaluating variability in the archaeological record of periods lacking such textual documentation.

## 2.4 Summary

By reframing the study of Mesoamerica based on key institutions and their articulation with one another, we allow for comparative analyses that consider multiple scales of human action, not simply views from the top of elite culture and governance structures. Scales intermediate between individual households and polities are particularly important for generating more nuanced social histories of the Mesoamerican past. The tension between the Nahua institutions of patron–client-type noble houses, such as the teccalli, and corporate-kin groups such as the calpolli is not simply a point of semantic debate, it illustrates a socio-structural conflict between more hierarchical and more heterarchical cultural institutions that affected the management of land and other key resources underlying the economies of Mesoamerican societies. It therefore connects the collective action frameworks relating to more local-level labor and resource issues covered by researchers such as Ostrom with the frameworks relating to polity-level fiscal and governance systems covered by researchers such as Levi. Somewhat like with the tensions between gumsa and gumlao within Kachin society, teccalli-like and calpolli-like social structures provide us with Indigenous institutions from Mesoamerica for considering variability in collective action in resource management and governance. With these better-documented institutions in mind, including their variability, we will now turn to earlier periods in Mesoamerican history, which have far fewer texts but offer millennia-long archaeological and iconographic records for evaluating known institutions through material remains.

## 3 Collective Action and Governance in the Mesoamerican Archaeological Record

Among the many pleasures of working as archaeologists in Mesoamerica are the opportunities to collaboratively study a wide array of cultural traditions with topical foci ranging from more specific historical concerns to broader social science ones. These topics span millennia and engage with big issues in early human history such as the origins of farming, urbanism, political evolution, and both the devastation and instances of resilience in the face of colonialism. Cultural institutions and their variability, detailed in part by the ethnographic and historic accounts reviewed in Section 2, serve as critical anchor points for archaeological reasoning employing material remains or the interpretation of prehispanic iconography and writing.

Cultural-historical details should not restrictively constrain how we think of prehispanic civilizations, since those societies existed for centuries or millennia prior to the thick descriptions of sixteenth-century texts and they inhabited a greater diversity of regions of Mesoamerica than are emphasized by such sources. Yet they can serve as correctives to tendencies within archaeology to apply models of social organization developed for other parts of the world or that draw from abstract social theory without considering actual known Indigenous institutions from Mesoamerica. They also help to counter the long-standing biases in Mesoamerican archaeology, iconography, and epigraphy resulting from analyzing seats of power, monuments, and art and text emphasizing political messaging and concerns of the elite class rather than conveying broader social history. Another current in the literature on Mesoamerica we would like to counter are narratives of urban or societal collapse that focus almost exclusively on environmental catastrophism, particularly events such as extended droughts or volcanic eruptions. Such studies are often published in prestigious science journals and are picked up by popular media outlets yet are often overly simplistic in highlighting some proposed correlation between environmental stress and collapse without considering counterfactual cases of episodes of stress that did not result in collapse, indicating that political and demographic declines were primarily multicausal processes that involved social stressors and some failure in the trust held for cultural institutions.

We mirror the organization of the first two sections here in dividing major themes relating to collective action in Mesoamerican archaeology into resource management and economies, which we review chronologically to also provide a sense of temporal changes, and issues relating more to governance and urbanism, which we do comparatively drawing on cases from urban societies from a few different time periods (Figure 13). Since we cannot be comprehensive, we select a sample of cases from different regions of Mesoamerica in order to illustrate the types of collective action problems people faced and how they responded to them similarly or differently over time. We emphasize variables relating to subsistence and urban infrastructure, iconographic and epigraphic

| Years | Western Mesoamerica | Eastern Mesoamerica | Macroregional Phenomena |
|---|---|---|---|
| 1500 | Late Postclassic | Late Postclassic | Aztec Empire |
| 1400 | Late Postclassic | Late Postclassic | Aztec Empire |
| 1300 | Middle Postclassic | | International style (Mixteca-Puebla) |
| 1200 | Middle Postclassic | Early Postclassic | International style (Mixteca-Puebla) |
| 1100 | Early Postclassic | Early Postclassic | Toltec style |
| 1000 | Early Postclassic | | Toltec style |
| 900 | | Terminal Classic | |
| 800 | Epiclassic | Late Classic | Classic Maya city-states |
| 700 | Epiclassic | Late Classic | Classic Maya city-states |
| 600 | | Late Classic | Classic Maya city-states |
| 500 | | Early Classic | |
| 400 | Classic | Early Classic | Teotihuacan |
| 300 | Classic | Early Classic | Teotihuacan |
| 200 | | Protoclassic | |
| CE 100 | Terminal Formative | | |
| CE 1 | Terminal Formative | Late Preclassic | Monte Albán |
| BCE 100 | Terminal Formative | Late Preclassic | Monte Albán |
| 200 | | Late Preclassic | |
| 300 | Late Formative | | multiregional urbanization |
| 400 | Late Formative | | multiregional urbanization |
| 500 | | Middle Preclassic | |
| 600 | Middle Formative | Middle Preclassic | |
| 700 | Middle Formative | Middle Preclassic | |
| 800 | Middle Formative | | |
| 900 | | | Olmec style |
| 1000 | | | |
| 1100 | Early Formative | Early Preclassic | |
| 1200 | Early Formative | Early Preclassic | |
| 1300 | | | early villages |
| 1400 | | | early villages |
| 1500 | | | early villages |

**Figure 13** Mesoamerican chronology between Archaic period and Spanish invasion, noting general differences between periodization in western and eastern Mesoamerica and selected macroregional phenomena.

content, uses of the calendar, the materialization of wealth inequality, and the relative size and longevity of urban centers. Drawing on previous studies (Carballo et al. 2022; Feinman and Carballo 2018, 2022; Feinman et al. 2023), we propose that urban centers in Mesoamerica featuring more collective or pluralistic institutions and greater investments in shared or public infrastructure tended to grow larger and last longer as central places relative to urban centers with more exclusive institutions and fewer infrastructural investments. Exceptions to this pattern exist in all regions and time periods, but the correlations are relatively strong and have implications not just for understanding prehispanic Mesoamerica but also for considering our future pathways as predominantly urban dwellers today.

## 3.1 Chronological Trends in Resource Management and Economies

Mesoamerica's transformation from being occupied mostly by mobile or seasonally mobile foraging populations to being occupied mostly by sedentary farmers residing in permanent villages unfolded over millennia of the Archaic period (ca. 8000–2000 BCE), extending into the Early Formative/Preclassic (ca. 2000–900/800 BCE) in several regions (Figure 14). The tempo was irregular and change was not unidirectional. The more ephemeral nature of traces of

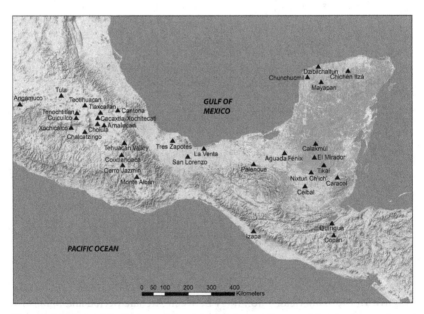

**Figure 14** Map with sites used in comparative analyses with others mentioned in the text.

occupation from this period and a long-standing research bias to more monumental centers dating from later periods make this early record spotty, but we can glean ways that people came together and shared in resource exploitation and labor from several sites. For instance, in the semiarid Valley of Oaxaca during the Middle Archaic period, sites such as Gheo-Shih attest to macroband gatherings of a few dozen people who camped together during the rainy season while collecting plant resources, perhaps sharing food, and demarcating "plaza" or "dance platform" space on the order of 140 m$^2$ bounded by parallel lines of boulders (Marcus and Flannery 1996: 52–59; see also Winter and Alarcón 2021: 306–308). In Archaic coastal settings featuring abundant marine resources, human intentionality in the formation of large shell mounds and the degree to which they were residentially occupied are debated points, with Clark and Hodgson (2021) proposing a more sedentary and intentional occupation for those located on the Soconusco coast. If accurate, these would represent pre-agricultural villages, some measuring up to 3.3 ha (33,000 m$^2$), with hypothesized houses along the edges of mounds that clustered around open community plazas. This proposal is admittedly speculative and in need of more investigation but, if one day confirmed, could represent cases of community cooperation in exploitation of a common-pool resource while simultaneously signaling to other groups, through the mass of mounded shell, their territorial claim to particularly productive mollusk beds.

With the development of farming based on maize and other crops, intentionality in communal labor becomes more archaeologically visible since it resulted in the landesque capital of hydraulic works, field systems, terrace networks, and other anthropogenic landscapes of subsistence infrastructure. Mesoamerica is an area of high climatological and microclimatic variability, but to generalize, farming in the semiarid highlands typically benefits from moving water to fields and terracing slopes to retain soil while farming in the humid lowlands typically benefits from moving water away from fields and houses during periods of inundation and diverting it to reservoirs. Reservoirs were also critical to communities in the southern Maya lowlands as sources of potable water during the dry season, since its karstic landscape means that groundwater is deeply buried. Wells were of limited utility except in select places with less porous substrates (Ashmore 1984; Lentz et al. 2015). The northern lowlands of the Yucatan Peninsula diverge from Mesoamerica's general highland/lowland ecologies in being semiarid and lacking rivers, so settlements clustered around subterranean water sources in the form of sinkholes (*cenotes*) and depressions (*rejolladas*). Groundwater levels are generally higher in highland settings, allowing potable water to be tapped through wells (Sanders et al. 1979: 221–293).

Understanding the socioeconomic relations that underlay any given case of subsistence infrastructure typically requires careful geoarchaeological research to establish their formation processes and chronology as well as accurate mapping of how people were distributed across the landscape and how households of varying statuses may have had disproportionate access to the resources. In areas that were riskier for crop failure, people were generally more incentivized to work together and buffer against risk, though relatively lush areas also offered potential gains to households that worked together in intensifying agricultural practices and it is clear that risk alone does not explain the distribution of subsistence infrastructure. As noted in Section 2, the lack of large domesticated animals in Mesoamerica meant that there were no true pastoral economies or plow-agriculture extensification of fields as drivers of differential wealth/land accumulation. Hunting and collecting activities remained relatively more important to Mesoamerican subsistence compared to early urban societies in Afro-Eurasia, providing other types of common-pool resources that were not privatized.

Starting in the lowlands, the expression of precocious art and early urbanism termed Olmec had a core in the humid southern Gulf Coast along seasonally inundated rivers such as the Coatzacoalcos, home to the monumental Early Preclassic center of San Lorenzo. To avoid flooding, the inhabitants of San Lorenzo created a patchwork of forty-seven elevated (1–5 m) residential mounds termed *islotes* that would have required concerted effort to build (Cyphers and Di Castro 2009). Mound construction was also directed at public spaces in San Lorenzo and subsequent La Venta, and both places exhibit a discernable sociopolitical hierarchy that emphasized individualized rule and elite differentiation through access to spot resources such as jade and iron ore, both procured through exchange from hundreds of kilometers away. Basaltic stone, used for sculptures expressing religious concepts and human power relations, was absent at these Olmec capitals and likewise needed to be imported. At San Lorenzo, more than 30 metric tons of stone was also sculpted to construct an elaborate covered drain or aqueduct running 170 m east–west (Coe and Diehl 1980: 118–127, fig. 83). The relatively short but elaborately built nature of the drain, its association with sculptures interpreted as water deities and aquatic fauna, and its association with small pools in central San Lorenzo are consistent with a ceremonial rather than a subsistence function, or as a means of providing potable water, and one that likely bolstered the power of San Lorenzo's ruling elite (Coe and Diehl 1980: 393). Contemporaneous with these Olmec sites, Middle Preclassic Maya communities began building earthen architecture on an equally monumental scale, with sites such as Aguada Fénix requiring an estimated 10–13 million person-days to construct (Inomata et al.

2020). Interestingly, Aguada Fénix and associated sites featuring colossal platforms and reservoir complexes were built by people who may have still retained patterns of seasonal mobility and did not exhibit notions of individualized rule in their art or as marked sociopolitical distinctions as did Gulf Olmec centers.

The Maya region is large and home to a range of strategies for subsistence infrastructure, including terraces in hilly regions like the Maya Mountains of

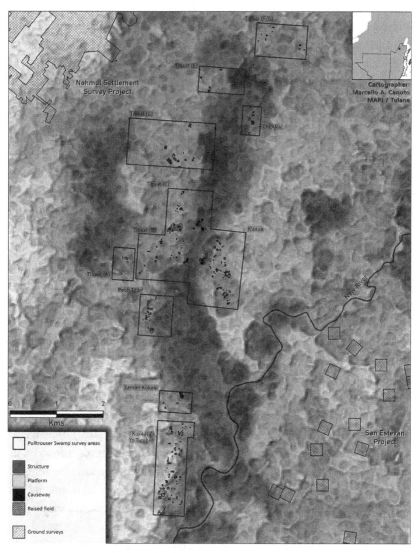

**Figure 15** Map of raised-field system in Pulltrouser Swamp, Belize, with associated Maya settlements. Map courtesy of Marcelo Canuto.

Belize, low-lying *bajos* in Guatemala's Peten district, irrigation in certain areas often as a means of creating reservoirs, and raised or drained fields in swampy areas (Fedick et al. 2023; Lentz et al. 2022; Palka 2023; Scarborough et al. 2012). The latter have been studied in detail in Pulltrouser Swamp (Figure 15), where raised-field construction was underway by the Late Preclassic and increased through the Late/Terminal Classic, eventually covering between 331 ha and 668 ha and likely allowing year-round cultivation (Turner and Harrison 2000: 247). By excavating canals on the mainland adjacent to the swamp, the Maya created channelized fields in depressed areas. Using the low estimate for total area, Turner and Harrison (2000: table 13-1) still extrapolate construction rates in the low thousands of days per hectare of the system, meaning a process that would have taken many years even if hundreds of workers participated in the undertaking. Household archaeology from the site of K'axob, adjacent to the raised fields at Pulltrouser Swamp, indicates that larger, more corporate households had longer occupations and more diversified economies, but bone-isotope analyses do not support the notion that local elites managed staple crop production and instead suggest this was managed by corporate-kin groups (Henderson 2003). Other Maya raised-field and reservoir systems have been mapped using LiDAR (light detection and ranging) (Beach et al. 2019; Hansen et al. 2022; Hutson et al. 2021) and are amenable to future research on how hydraulic infrastructure was organized, whether as common-pool resources or as more privatized, toll-goods systems benefiting an elite class. In cases of the large Classic period Maya cities, the reservoir systems of centers such as Tikal may have been elite-managed and incorporated into rituals of royal aggrandizement, while more decentralized systems, such as with terraces at Caracol and other sites, afforded opportunities for neighborhood-level collective action and more bottom-up management processes (Lentz et al. 2022).

In addition to diverting water from inundated areas to create dry land, bringing water to crops, and storing water for drinking, lowland Maya water-scapes also included the purposeful cultivation of freshwater fisheries containing species of fish, turtles, crustaceans, and mollusks (Palka 2023). If managed sustainably, such species would have provided dependable protein sources, as well as field fertilizer, in a similar fashion to the lacustrine environments of highland Mesoamerica and may have similarly been managed as common-pool resources by social groups intermediate between households and states. The maintenance of aquatic landscapes, both natural and anthropogenic, was therefore a key collective action issue for lowland Mesoamerican populations. In some cases, their contamination may have been observable by ancestral Maya populations and adapted to, as appears to have been the case with the creation of sand filtration systems in certain reservoirs (Lentz et al. 2015, 2022; Scarborough et al. 2012). In others, such as with sedimentation processes resulting from deforestation and urban-waste runoff near lowland lakes, the centuries-long unfolding of water contamination may have been difficult to notice or adapt to, leading to population decline (Birkett et al. 2023).

Management of water and soil resources in the Mesoamerican highlands differed from that of the lowlands in several ways, including the construction of more terrace networks to flatten land on hillier terrain, more canal irrigation systems to deal with semiarid precipitation regimes, fewer reservoirs for potable water since groundwater could typically be tapped through wells, and less mounding of earth into dry land since inundation is less of a concern. These nevertheless reflect general trends and it is clear that highlanders and lowlanders were both familiar with this range of subsistence infrastructure that they could adapt to a particular ecological setting when appropriate. In the highlands, the construction of some of these forms of subsistence infrastructure began during the Archaic period, but they became more pervasive during the Middle Formative (900–500 BCE) associated with agricultural intensification and the rise of nascent urban centers.

A form of land-making analogous to what was practiced in the lowlands can be seen in the tlateles constructed along lake margins of the Basin of Mexico (Cordova 2022; Cordova et al. 2022). Unlike with the longer and more linear chinampas, tlateles functioned as residential platforms and were therefore constructed with more proportionally sized square or rectangular sides, though the two types of land-making shared similarities in using palisaded enclosures of wooden stakes and lattice to retain sediments (Cordova 2022: 195–214). Tlateles ranged in area from tens of square meters – suitable for a dwelling or two and necessitating only household labor – to hundreds of square meters, similar in scale to the islotes of Gulf Olmec settlements and necessitating suprahousehold labor. In both cases, however, a primary driver for tlatel construction was lake aquaculture, including the harvesting of common-pool resources such as fish, algae, salt, aquatic birds, and other lake fauna.

Irrigation networks began with Archaic maize agriculture in the highlands but proliferated during the Middle Formative (Doolittle 1990; Nichols et al. 2006). These could be fed by springs that provided water throughout the year in select locations or by branching off canals from rivers and seasonal streams near lakeshores or seasonal wetlands termed humedales, as was the case in the ethnographic example from southern Tlaxcala documented by Wilken (1968). In this same area millennia earlier, drained-field systems were constructed by the inhabitants of the large regional center of Xochitecatl at the confluence of the two major rivers of the Puebla-Tlaxcala Valley (Serra Puche et al. 2004). An

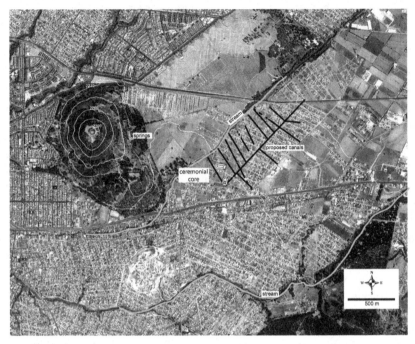

**Figure 16** The Formative town of Amalucan, with its irrigation network, ceremonial core of mounds, and isolated mound on Cerro Amalucan. Map based on Fowler (1987) overlay on 2001 satellite image from Google Earth. Today the site is almost completely covered by Puebla's urban sprawl.

example of a modest, community-sized system was documented at Amalucan, today on the outskirts of the contemporary city of Puebla (Fowler 1987). This Middle to Late Formative network of canals was fed by springs and seasonal streams (Figure 16). The settlement grew to be a large town of the period, covering some 10 km², but began more modestly, with an irrigation system providing water to an estimated 1,000 ha of fields and later temple construction covering some of these earlier canals – a stratigraphic indication that the estimated 80,000 m³ of earth moved for excavating the canals was accomplished prior to the development of a more hierarchical political-religious system. The inhabitants of the larger cities of Cuicuilco and Teotihuacan created more extensive irrigation and reservoir networks drawing on nearby springs (Figure 17) and, particularly in the case of Teotihuacan, situated in the more arid northern Basin of Mexico, dug canals on the slopes of nearby mountains to capture rain water and humidify fields prior to planting once rains became more consistent (Evans and Nichols 2015; Sanders et al. 1979: 230–260).

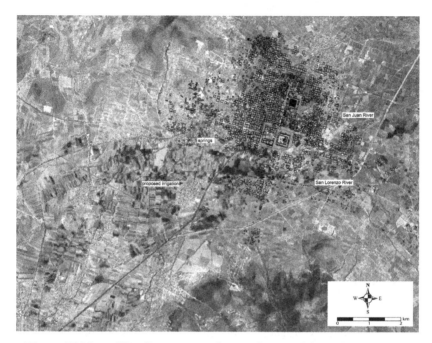

**Figure 17** Map of Teotihuacan superimposed over a false-color composite LANDSAT satellite image that highlights currently vegetated areas southwest of the city at the confluence of the San Juan and San Lorenzo rivers and where springs provide water for permanent irrigation.

These Formative and Classic period hydraulic systems have their origins in strategies developed earlier in the more arid Tehuacán Valley of southern Puebla, where irrigation networks were created in tandem with maize cultivation during the Archaic period. Neely and colleagues (2022) draw on the work of Ostrom (e.g., 1990) in documenting five prehispanic irrigation networks in Tehuacán that were all substantially larger than Amalucan's, ranging from 825 ha to 3,852 ha of estimated irrigation farmland, and all constructed by smaller-scale communities that do not exhibit signs of any coercive authority to organize the labor. Yet the most impressive hydraulic project from Tehuacán was the construction of the Purrón Dam Complex during the Early and Middle Formative period as a means of creating a reservoir to feed the irrigation systems. At its largest extent during the Middle Formative, the complex comprised some 390,000 m$^3$ of construction volume, creating an estimated reservoir volume of nearly a million cubic meters of water (Neely et al. 2015) (Figure 18). It is therefore centuries earlier and larger than the dam and reservoir systems at Maya cities such as El Mirador, extrapolated thus far based on LiDAR mapping (Hansen et al. 2022), and Tikal, which have been documented through

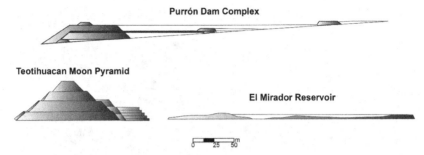

**Figure 18** To-scale renderings of the Purrón Dam Complex, Moon Pyramid at Teotihuacan, and El Mirador (La Jarilla) reservoir. Redrawn from Neely et al. (2015: fig. 4), Sugiyama and López Luján (2007: fig. 1), and Hansen et al (2022: fig. 21).

Unfilled lines for Purrón and Mirador indicate the water capacity of reservoirs. Note that the largest construction of the Purrón Dam stretches some 400 m wide, not visible in cross-section, whereas the base of the Moon Pyramid is square.

excavations and geoarchaeological investigations as well (Scarborough et al. 2012). The construction volume of the Purrón Dam Complex is also significantly larger than the volume of Teotihuacan's Moon Pyramid or any of the largest pyramidal temple platforms of Formative period central Mexico (Carballo 2016; Murakami 2015). Hydraulic projects from the Tehuacán Valley should therefore serve as an example to global archaeology of the possibilities for large-scale collective action on the part of small-scale societies lacking the trappings of significant sociopolitical hierarchy such as elaborate palaces or elite tombs. We hope it serves as a nail in the coffin to facile notions of monumental constructions requiring state or other hierarchical oversight.

Irrigation systems were also constructed farther south in the southern highlands of Oaxaca, but here we will instead emphasize the region's terrace networks, which were built on slopes to flatten living surfaces, to retain soil and moisture for plant cultivation, or some combination of the two. In Oaxaca's smaller valley systems, Zapotec and Mixtec communities developed a characteristic mode of urbanism of terraced hilltowns, which can be defined as a coherent "type" of Mesoamerican settlement that was especially enduring in the region (Kowalewski et al. 2006). Frontal terrace walls were generally shared by multiple residential units and drains often were situated in the narrow spaces between individual terraces, requiring neighboring families to coordinate labor for their construction and maintenance. At the base of residential sectors, networks of interconnected terraces known as *lama-bordo* are cross-channel irrigation systems and provide a clear example of a common-pool

**Figure 19** Aerial photo of the long-lived hilltown and Zapotec capital city of Monte Albán.

resource that require sustained cooperation at the suprahousehold level, as dereliction in maintenance on the part of one family would have negative consequences on others, particularly associated with downslope erosion (Pérez Rodríguez 2016).

Serving as the Zapotec capital city for some 1,250 years, Monte Albán was the most prominent and longest lived Oaxacan hilltown, eventually being enmeshed in a network of more than 2,000 terraces along with fortification walls that protected certain slopes (Figure 19) (Blanton et al. 2022; Marcus and Flannery 1996: 139–154; Nicholas and Feinman 2022). During the initial mapping of the city, a range of civic hydraulic features were documented that include drains, dams, canals, and pools (O'Brien et al. 1980). More recent investigations have documented the presence of a spring located at the bottom of the northeast slope of Monte Albán, approximately 1 km from the urban epicenter and emanating from the hill itself. Water was channelized into a series of canals and pools, and the flow of water from the hilltown may have given Monte Albán a symbolic identification with a water-mountain (Martínez Gracida 2017), like many other Mesoamerican cities and urban monuments.

In addition to the world of subsistence resources, visible archaeologically through various types of infrastructure or landesque capital, was the Mesoamerican world of goods that circulated through various networks of patronage and commercialized exchange and is generally visible through the record of portable artifacts. Blanton, Fargher, and Heredia (2005; Blanton and Fargher 2012) have outlined a useful classification for major types of goods within Mesoamerica and other premodern economies: (1) regional goods, the backbone of any system of economic exchange, tending to be widely available to non-elites and more "utilitarian" in nature; (2) prestige goods, tending to be exclusive to elites, more "symbolic" in nature, and made from rare materials and/or with labor-added value; (3) bulk luxury goods, existing somewhere between regional and prestige goods in being rarer or more elaborate but also available to non-elites through greater commercialization of economies and more robust market circulation. In very broad terms, the three millennia of precolonial Mesoamerican history, from its first villages to the Spanish invasion, can be characterized by three major episodes in the relative import of these types of goods. The Early–Middle Formative Olmec interaction sphere saw a prioritization of prestige goods as status markers during processes of developing sociopolitical hierarchies. The Late Formative through Classic periods was marked by an intensification of regional goods production and circulation, as urban centers flourished in most parts of Mesoamerica, creating more scalar economies, tax/tribute structures, and early markets. In some cases, like with Thin Orange pottery at Teotihuacan, forms of bulk luxuries circulated widely, but this intensified during the Postclassic period with the intensification of markets, professional merchant classes, and political confederations like the Aztec Triple Alliance promoting relatively open exchange across political boundaries (Hirth 2016: 188–236).

Major transformations and axes of variation in Mesoamerican economies can then be connected with collective action frameworks and known cultural institutions by considering what types of production and circulation activities would have been more exclusionary, concentrated disproportionately in the hands of social elites, versus those that would have been more inclusive, with greater accessibility to finished products on the part of non-elites and potential profits to be made on the part of intermediate-scale social groups such as cooperating households or guild-like corporate economic groups. The intensification of regional goods economies during the Late Formative to Classic, such as the wider circulation of mass-produced pottery and obsidian blades, and of bulk luxuries during the Postclassic, such as the wide availability of polychrome pottery, cacao, and cotton textiles, engendered new socioeconomic relations and networks among Mesoamericans (Blanton et al. 2005;

Feinman et al. 2022). Much of the resource management of these craft production systems and the distribution of goods through corporate trading groups who operated semi-autonomously from polities (e.g., the pochteca) would be classed as toll goods in schema like Figure 2, generally of lower analytical interest since their management dynamics are more privatized and therefore relatively straightforward. However, the political maintenance of the market systems and open trade routes that circulated these goods could be viewed as a public good to consumers, with a social contract of urban/state taxation to keep the flow of goods moving, like the schema in Figure 12. Together with the subsistence economy and its associated infrastructure, the variable emphases in types of goods formed the foundations of political economies and the fiscal streams of governance. These foundations had both material and ideological components.

## 3.2 Governance and Ideologies of Inclusion and Exclusion

The interactions between different nested scales of subsistence and economic resources reviewed in previous sections, the definition of users permitted to harness and consume them, and the cultural institutions and governing structures involved in their management created a diversity of urban and political arrangements in early Mesoamerica. We can draw from the textually documented institutions from later periods, covered in Section 2, to build interpretive frameworks that allow for consideration of a similar range of diversity both regionally and temporally. Our dataset here includes variables such as how individuals arranged themselves residentially, coordinated group action at intermediate scales between households and entire settlements, worked together to create shared infrastructure and other undertakings, organized their urban centers, and expressed difference in wealth, power, and other aspects of social identity. These choices and actions were enmeshed within cognitive systems of religious belief and political ideology, which shared some core elements across Mesoamerica but also varied over space and time.

Returning to Kirchoff's (1943) early formulation of Mesoamerica as a culture area, calendrical systems provided broadly shared means of parsing time and synchronizing group activities, including ritual cycles and organizing communal labor. The Calendar Round pairing of a 365-day solar year and 260-day ritual year is a culturally distinctive attribute of Mesoamerican cultures that appears to have had its origins at the same time as the coordinating of hydraulic projects in the Early–Middle Formative period reviewed in Section 3.1. Hieroglyphic dates clearly establish the use of the calendar later in the Formative, but recent analysis of solar alignments from Aguada Fénix and other Middle Formative platform complexes of the Usumacinta region show an earlier interest in charting 260-day intervals within the 365-day solar year (Šprajc et al. 2023). It includes one site of interest, La Carmelita, with alignments to sunset on April 30 and August 13, a splitting of the solar year into 260/105-day intervals that became canonical in central Mexico during the Classic period as major alignments for Teotihuacan and Cholula but was present in the region during the later Formative at sites such as Totimehuacan (Carballo and Aveni 2012). In the case of central Mexico, the division might correlate with the agricultural year, parsing much of the rainy season from the dry season. Of the Middle Formative Usumacinta platforms, Šprajc and colleagues (2023: 9) observe: "These constructions possibly symbolized a sense of attachment to fixed localities and provided concrete images of communal collaboration that could be shared among the growing populations."

Although the Mesoamerican calendar was a strongly shared means of coordinating time, it was employed differently regionally and temporally and could be used more inclusively or more exclusively. In other words, this cultural institution of reconciling solar and human cycles, the Calendar Round, could intersect differently with other institutions, such as political ones (i.e., to legitimate rule) or economic ones (i.e., to time markets or redistributive festivals). Drawing on ethnographic examples from Maya communities in the highlands of Guatemala and ethnohistoric examples from sixteenth-century central Mexico, Brumfiel (2011) distinguishes between more exclusive (elite-focused) and inclusive (non-elite-focused) uses of the calendar in Aztec pottery, sculpture, and codices. Whereas relatively more exclusionary or politicized uses of the calendar included state-sponsored sacrificial rituals, tax and tribute from conquered polities, and the training of a predominantly elite class through the calmecac, ethnohistoric texts and calendrical motifs on the bulk-luxury of Aztec polychrome vessels evince widespread knowledge of the functioning of the calendar by non-elites and their differential uses for suprahousehold alliance building through consumption events relating to lifecycle rituals.

Teotihuacan's writing system was a clear precursor to Aztec writing, dating more than a millennium earlier and possibly representing an earlier Nahua or at least Uto-Aztecan language, but the corpus of hieroglyphs is much smaller, currently numbering fewer than 400 documented examples (Helmke and Nielsen 2021; Whittaker 2021). Nevertheless, more than half of these come from ceramic vessels and a better cataloging of provenience, when available, could elucidate whether these circulated through more inclusive or more exclusive networks, akin to Brumfiel's study of Aztec ceramics. What is clear, however, is that Teotihuacanos employed Calendar Round dates and emphasized naming places (toponyms) or buildings, social roles of people (i.e., offices) over individuals, and cosmological narratives that paired such text labels with imagery. The importance of the Calendar Round at Teotihuacan is apparent not only through its hieroglyphs and urban planning but also through a characteristic symbol the pecked cross, which often feature 260 dots and divisions thereof carved into stone and the floors of buildings as a highly legible representation of the ritual calendar. Of more than seventy examples documented in Mesoamerica, most have been found at Teotihuacan and the city's hinterland (Aveni 2005, 2010). The symbol's attributes "leave little doubt that practical elements related to the seasonal calendar and its relationship to the sacred count are extant in the petroglyphs" (Aveni 2005: 43). We agree with Aveni and others that this Teotihuacano emphasis on broad dissemination of the Calendar Round was a means of sharing a time–space cosmovision with other parts of Mesoamerica linked to the city's intensification of exchange networks (Figure 20), many emphasizing regional goods, and promotion of periodic markets (Feinman and Carballo 2022; Feinman and Nicholas 2020a).

Classic Maya writing evolved to be the most sophisticated written communication of the precolonial Americas and was capable of visibly recording any element of speech. Nevertheless, the writing system was applied disproportionately as a means of recording dynastic history and of aggrandizing elite individuals, especially the *k'uhl ajaw* or "holy blood lords" who emerged as powerful

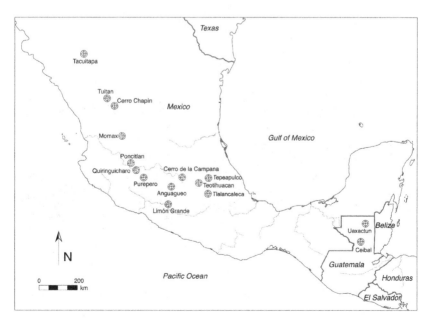

**Figure 20** Map with distribution of Teotihuacan-style pecked crosses in Mesoamerica.

monarchs during the Late Classic period (Marcus 1992; Martin 2020). The individualizing emphasis of Classic Maya writing included use of the Long Count calendar as a means of more precisely recording time, largely to the end of situating the actions of powerful people within it, as well as statements of authorship of texts and ownership of the materials labeled by texts. These emphases are seen in the writing of many of the most powerful Classic Maya capitals, but it is also important to note the variability in the use of writing across the territorially extensive Maya world, with some meaningful axes between the northern and southern lowlands and between more urban and rural settlements (Hutson 2016; Hutson et al. 2021; Robin 2013). Nonetheless, in the aggregate the emphases of writing in capital cities differ significantly from how Teotihuacanos wrote in several respects, including thematically, spatially, and in terms of broad legibility (Table 3) (Feinman and Carballo 2022).

Significant differences in the iconography of Teotihuacan and Classic Maya capitals are also apparent and mirror differences observed in writing systems in conveying cosmological narratives that share elements of Mesoamerican belief but apply them in relatively more inclusive or exclusive ways. Teotihuacan famously has no unambiguous depictions of paramount rulers, while these are abundant in Classic Maya capitals.

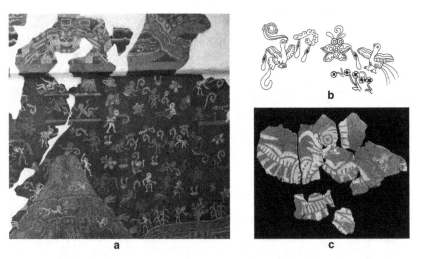

a                              c

**Figure 21** Photos of murals from Teotihuacan depicting types of paradises: (a) portion of a watery paradise from Tepantitla, with non-elites frolicking in a water mountain, tending to irrigated fields, and dancing and playing among butterflies, with the Storm God floating above; portions of a flowery paradise with bird, butterfly, and flower motifs from (b) the center of the city (Palace of the Sun) and (c) the urban periphery (Tlajinga).

**Table 3** Comparative trends among communication systems of Teotihuacan and Classic Maya capitals.

| Integrative/ Communication Technologies | Teotihuacan | Classic Maya Capitals |
| --- | --- | --- |
| Writing | Short texts primarily serving as tags or labels, often large format (murals), not linguistic | Many texts on diverse media with emphasis on elite individuals, often small format, exclusive audience, linguistic (average longer length of text) |
| Murals/symbols | Domestic contexts, cosmological themes, no personal ownership labels | Restrictive spaces, portable goods in elite networks, individual ownership labels |
| Calendar | "Open-access" short-term cyclic calendars – fosters broad participation in calendric rituals, market rounds | Long count – precise, restricted, scholarly |
| Public spaces | Large, more accessible | Small, restricted |
| Intra-settlement movement | Grid plan, wide thoroughfares | Spoke-wheel (all paths to center of community) |
| Education | Possible schools – qualified by class and ability (Aztec analogy) | Elite scribal training |
| Ritual | Depictions of ritual activities involving coordinated movements of priests and warriors | Depictions of ruler spectacles, royal bloodletting, shamanistic transformation into powerful animal spirits |
| Decorated pottery | Cosmological themes | Representations of courts, rulers |

Teotihuacano art emphasizes themes of collective concern, such as agricultural abundance, cosmic renewal, and military might, and when humans are depicted they are typically done so as social roles and subordinated only to deities, such as in the Tepantitla mural where priests are subordinated to a deity and non-elites frolic in a paradise of butterflies, flowering trees, and a water-mountain feeding irrigated fields (Figure 21(a)). Flowery paradises associated with the afterlife and ancestors were widespread in art and religious narratives of Mesoamerica and adjacent culture areas, but we again see important differences among Classic Maya capitals, where it was primarily associated with rulers and royal lineages, and Teotihuacan, where it was primarily associated with militarism and a glorious death associated with valor in the battlefield (Turner and Mathiowetz 2021). That such a flowery paradise was accessible to non-elite warriors at Teotihuacan is supported by the fact that its related iconography was broadly disseminated in mass-produced portable art, such as composite censers, and used as mural decoration in neighborhood centers on the urban periphery of the city among its lower socioeconomic stratum (Figure 21(c)) (Carballo et al. 2021). Some sort of pathway to quasi-elite status through warfare at Teotihuacan, analogous to the Eagle Nobles of Aztec society (see Table 2), is certainly possible, but we can also draw on collective military ideologies among the Greek poleis, Roman Republic, and other cases of more pluralistic polities outside Mesoamerica.

Importantly, as with long-lived Eurasian polities like Rome, governing structures and ideologies of inclusion/exclusion changed through time in Mesoamerican polities. The more individualizing foci of Maya writing and visual communication emerged and declined with the Classic period, especially the Late Classic. For the most part, political messaging of the Preclassic and Postclassic periods appears very different and likely indicates broad shifts in models of governance of the sort reviewed ethnohistorically in Section 2.3 (see Eberl et al. 2023). In some cases, due to the richness of textual and iconographic evidence, we can perceive such shifts between more exclusive and more inclusive governance at the timescale of years rather than centuries. Such is the case from the ornately sculpted city of Copán, which suffered a devastating blow to the polity when the long and prosperous reign of its thirteenth ruler, Waxaklajun Ub'ah K'awil, ended by this dynast being captured and killed in 738 CE by a former vasal city-state Quirigua. When Copán's fourteenth ruler took the throne, his strategy appears to have been to more broadly share power among noble families, depicting their leaders on the façade of a council house – the *Popol Na* or "Mat House," with the mat representing a symbol of rulership (Figure 22) (Fash 2001: 130–134). This shift to a more pluralistic or oligarchic

**Figure 22** Photo of the council House (*Popol Na*), with sculpted mat motifs and hieroglyphs, from the Maya city of Copán, Honduras.

system of governance at Copán, associated with a period of political turmoil and the erection of a purposefully deliberative building, was relatively short-lived as the monarchy reestablished itself and next commissioned the longest hieroglyphic text known from the precolonial Americas in commemoration of its dynastic line of succession.

> Ruler 14's apparent response was to draw in his governors and lords to a public meeting house, to portray them prominently on the building's façade, and pay homage to their role in their communities', and the state's future. Of considerable interest is that Ruler 14 did not place his own portrait on a stela in front of the building itself. This decentralized approach was later to be greatly over-shadowed by the works of his successors. (Fash 2001: 134)

In her study of Classic Maya political dynamics, Foias (2013: 192–197) considers the revenue streams of various polities, along the spectrum presented by authors such as Levi (1988) and Blanton and Fargher (2008). She proposes that externally derived, prestige resources were critical to palace economies but that tax/tribute systems drew more on internal resources, which is logical given the difficulties in moving bulk goods long distances in prehispanic Mesoamerica. Foias proposes that council houses such as Copán's could serve as important buffers to the power of dynasts during the Late Classic period and proliferated during the Terminal Classic, leading to the more pluralistic systems seen in places such as Chichén Itzá and elsewhere. Maya council houses were "another power bloc that would have competed with the other political factions of the k'uhul ajaw (divine lords), non-royal aristocrats, priests, and warriors (although there may have been some overlap between these groups)" (Foias 2013: 197). Such a multiscalar perspective that considers the motivations and relative agency of various factions – different noble lineages, suprahousehold corporate groups, and varied subalterns – moves us beyond simplistic debates in Mesoamerican archaeology that consider governance primarily or exclusively in terms of the structure of paramount rulers. The rich array of formations from later periods provide us with culturally meaningful parameters for interpreting earlier cases in the archaeological record.

Efforts to systematically compare Mesoamerican cities and settlements have been revived over the last decade or two following earlier attempts associated with the boom in regional studies of the 1960s–1970s and a subsequent decline during the 1980s–1990s. Some of the revival relates to new geospatial technologies applied to archaeology, such as geographic information systems (GIS) and remote-sensing, and some comes from cross-disciplinary borrowing from fields such as political science, economics, sociology, cultural demography, and urban studies. Examples include attempts to quantify socioeconomic inequality using Gini indices (e.g., Kohler and Smith 2018), to understand relationships between scales of settlement and various societal phenomena (e.g., Ortman et al. 2014), and to create global databases of cultural-historical variables for comparative analyses (e.g., Turchin et al. 2013). In all cases, judgment calls must be made on the part of regional specialists and collaborators in order to fit various complex and dynamic phenomena into much simpler and more static categories. They do not deal well with micro-historical shifts like we just discussed at Copán or saw earlier among Tenochtitlan's rulers. Nevertheless, if the data are recorded and reported transparently they can be debated, modified, and improved for new iterations of such analyses.

It is in this spirit of comparative analyses as works in progress that we have collaborated with other colleagues on studies of urban centers in Mesoamerica focusing on issues of systems of governance, communication, economies, inequality, infrastructure, and the intersection of these in relation to the longevity of settlements as central places (Carballo et al. 2022; Feinman and Carballo 2018, 2022; Feinman et al. 2023). Durable infrastructure of the sort we have been referencing throughout this Element – irrigation systems, terraces, roads, neighborhood public spaces, and the like – can be viewed as materialized consensus among the households that built, maintained, and benefited from such projects (Smith 2016). In many cases, who benefited and what sorts of consensus was reached can be difficult to discern in the absence of text, with land tenure and subcommunity-level irrigation systems being two prominent examples. Yet when people shared physical walls between residences, terraces,

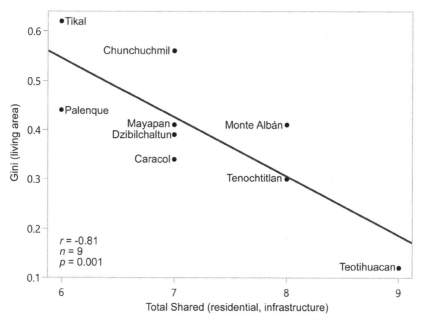

**Figure 23** Graph depicting negative correlation between calculated Gini score, measured by living area, and ordinal scale of shared residential and neighborhood space for a sample of nine Mesoamerican cities, indicating that those with more shared space tend also to be more equal. For sources, see Carballo et al. (2022).

access-ways, or social infrastructure within neighborhoods, some bonds of interdependence would have been necessary.

To evaluate the relationship between shared infrastructure and broader societal dynamics we coded a sample of Mesoamerican urban centers in the publications reviewed thus far based on variables of housing and shared/social infrastructure. For housing, we created a scale of 1–4 in degrees of shared space from isolated houses, patio-groups, agglutinated house compounds, and larger apartment compounds, of which only Teotihuacan had as the dominant housing type. For shared infrastructure, we created a binary scale (0 or 1) of walls, terraces, roads, plazas, temples, and other presumed civic buildings present or absent at the scale of neighborhoods, giving a total range of 0–6 and a total ordinal scale of 0–10, adding residences. Figure 23 illustrates the statistically significant negative correlation between the shared infrastructure of a sample of nine Mesoamerican centers with published Gini coefficients and detailed site maps amendable to assessing types of urban infrastructure.

Although the sample is admittedly small, and the results should be taken as preliminary, it suggests that urban centers with more shared infrastructure were more equitable than those with less shared infrastructure. For this analysis, we wanted to include shared residential space because that variable is the primary determinant of calculating Gini coefficients in comparative literature, but we acknowledge that this variable alone poses problems. When it comes to housing value, as any realtor will tell you, location matters, and as any contractor will tell you, the quality of construction materials matters. A more accurate evaluation of inequality in household archaeology would therefore include consideration of location and labor invested in construction, but this complicates comparative analysis across world regions at larger scales. We have therefore also used other indices of inequality such as household goods (Feinman et al. 2018). Likewise, infrastructure could better be quantified as a continuous rather than an ordinal variable – for instance, linear meters of terracing per person in a settlement – but this also adds to the time cost of comparative analyses. Nevertheless, the correlation highlights some of the variables of urban living that have been documented as unique or relatively unusual, such as apartment living organized around neighborhood centers with the properties of institutions like the later calpolli or tlaxilacalli at Teotihuacan (Cabrera Castro and Gómez Chávez 2008; Manzanilla 2017).

For a second analysis, we examined the relationship between shared infrastructure and the longevity of a larger sample of Mesoamerican urban centers. We define longevity here as the duration in years that a given center was at approximately half or greater its estimated maximal population and we omitted any Postclassic centers whose trajectories were truncated by the Spanish invasion. For settlements that had two discrete periods of occupation with population estimates and maps with architecture, such as Cerro Jazmín, we separated them as two urban centers, whereas those with multiple occupation periods but featuring population estimates and/or architectural reconstructions for just one of them we used only a single apogee of occupation score. For this analysis, we only consider shared neighborhood infrastructure, not residence type, which we wanted for the analysis of Gini values based on living area. Figure 24 illustrates the statistically significant positive correlation between apogee length and shared infrastructure in a sample of twenty urban centers. The two analyses together are consistent with a broader literature in urban studies and related fields on positive-feedback loops between iterated interactions among neighbors and that initial civic investments in shared infrastructure can promote sustained social capital needed for larger-scale collective action in more equitable

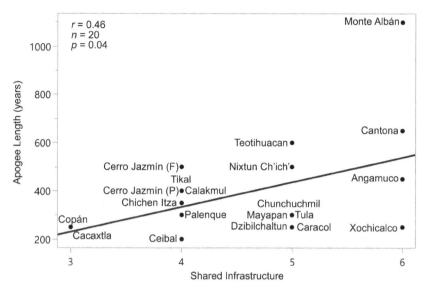

**Figure 24** Graph depicting a positive correlation between apogee length and an ordinal scale of shared neighborhood infrastructure for a sample of twenty Mesoamerican cities. Cerro Jazmín's two separated occupations are coded as Formative and Postclassic. For data sources, see Carballo et al. (2022).

and resilient social formations (e.g., Jensen and Ramey 2020; Klinenberg 2018; McGhee 2021).

We also queried the relationships between other variables that were not correlated in our sample of urban centers. For instance, the relationship between total population of an urban center and its longevity is close to random ($r = 0.02$, $p = 0.91$ for 27 cases). A positive correlation does exist between population density and apogee length, but it is not statistically significant ($r = 0.37$, $p = 0.57$ for 27 cases). However, when we classified urban centers along an ordinal scale of relative degrees of collectivity following the axes summarized in Table 1 we discovered stronger correlations. For this scale, we coded inputs along three domains of political economy (internal vs. external fiscal finance, levels of socioeconomic inequality), governance (more pluralistic vs. more autocratic), and architecture (levels of accessibility to public space and infrastructure, centrality of palaces) to rank levels of collectivity in sociopolitical organization (see Carballo et al. 2022; Feinman and Carballo 2018). Using this scale, we see a stronger correlation between total population and collectivity ($r = 0.29$, $p = 0.14$ for 27 cases), though still not statistically significant, yet we register a highly significant ($p = 0.01$) positive correlation between collectivity and apogee length (Figure 25). Taken

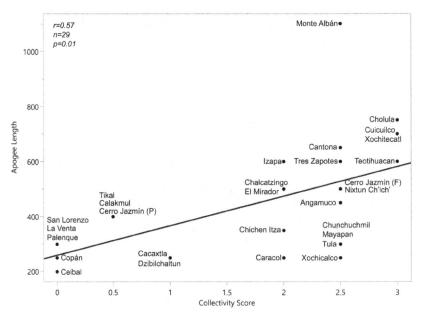

**Figure 25** Graph depicting positive correlation between apogee length and an ordinal scale of collectivity in internal sociopolitical organization for a sample of twenty-seven Mesoamerican cities. Cerro Jazmín's two separated occupations are coded as Formative and Postclassic. For data sources, see Carballo et al. (2022) and Feinman and Carballo (2018).

together, these analyses indicate that sociopolitical organization, rather than population measures, was the key variable in the resilience and longevity of urban centers in early Mesoamerica.

While these analyses of macroscale patterns in urban centers are illuminating, all the cases listed in Figures 23–25 eventually suffered declines, and prehispanic Mesoamerica also offers contemporary lessons relating to different forms of societal collapse and reconfiguration. Climatic stressors, particularly relating to extended drought and unpredictability in annual precipitation, are frequently proposed as primary drivers of collapse without much consideration of historical variables and counterfactual cases of periods of climate stress that did not result in collapse. When paleoclimate data are combined with detailed analyses of cultural and historical variables in more interdisciplinary studies, the conclusions are much more nuanced and compelling (see especially Hoggarth et al. 2017). Ultimately, we see crises in social trust to be the key variable determining whether polities endure through perturbations stemming from environmental forces, factionalism, or macro-socioeconomic processes, whether their governance structure lies at the more pluralistic or more autocratic end of the spectrum (e.g., Golden and Sherer 2013; Manzanilla 2015). Trust is the social glue that keeps collective action and large societal formations together (Levi 1996; Ostrom and Walker 2003). Collective labor as implemented through shared infrastructure is a powerful means of fostering trust and interpersonal ties both with coresidents and neighbors. When implemented effectively, it can generate virtuous cycles and sustained positive outcomes. Yet declines in trust undermine the social contracts that underpin contributions to the institutional systems responsible for public goods dissemination. As is expected from the relationships outlined in the schematic rendering of Figure 12, such breakdowns are capable of undermining the interpersonal and institutional networks necessary to keep the system going, resulting in enough people rejecting it and so leading to collapse.

In the central and southern highlands of Mesoamerica, the collapses of Teotihuacan and Monte Albán appear to be related to the compromising of more collective political arrangements by patron–client systems centered on noble houses (Feinman and Nicholas 2016; Manzanilla 2015). The polities that arose in the wake of their decline – such as Cacaxtla, Xochicalco, and Zaachila – exhibit more exclusive and individualizing art and architecture, including the greater centrality of palaces and noble genealogies. In central Mexico in particular, Teotihuacan remained a powerful touchstone for claims to political legitimacy through the Aztec period (Carrasco et al. 2000). Teotihuacan's collapse may have also affected developments in Oaxaca, leading to state balkanization into patron–client systems that distributed the more centralized authority of Monte Albán. Yet the city continued in the historical memory of Zapotec and Mixtec peoples as a powerful place, serving as a necropolis and referenced in Postclassic codices (Feinman and Nicholas 2016; Jansen and Pérez Jiménez 2011: 317–327). Historical memory of these powerful places is likely part of the moral rhetoric of good governance recorded in oral histories like the huehuehtlahtolli passage from Section 2.3. It likely contributed to developing the Toltec and later Aztec "syntheses" in central Mexico and their related pan-Mesoamerican interaction spheres known as the "international style" or Postclassic world-system, associated with the institutions we reviewed from historically documented periods.

## 3.3 Summary

In this necessarily cursory review of millennia of Mesoamerican history, we hope to have highlighted several ways in which interpretive frameworks grounded in collective action theory and drawing on established cultural institutions from the ethnographic and ethnohistoric record can recast investigations on major issues relating to variability in societal organization over time and place. The triangulation between the archaeological record, documented cultural intuitions, and broader social theory, often called the direct-historical approach, has a long history of debate in Americanist archaeology (Lyman and O'Brien 2001; Wylie 1985). When applied with too heavy a hand, it can serve to stifle evidence of change over time, something that is clearly observable in the archaeological record. We see the benefits of the approach taken here to include the setting of reasonable parameters for the institutions and strategies that past peoples were likely to have pursued at varied scales of interaction in a way capable of considering human agency and change through time. Frameworks for collective action and governance informed by a diversity of plausible cultural institutions shed new light on how elements of Mesoamerican societies considered canonical to defining the culture region from early definitions such as Kirchhoff's (1943) – subsistence strategies, parsing time, regional economies, urban life, governance – varied based on differing strategies for human–environment interactions across the spectrum of socioeconomic status, political power, cultural identities, and other axes of human variability.

Forms of collective action can be detected from some of the earliest chapters of Mesoamerican history, documented archaeologically in cooperative subsistence activities and gatherings as part of forager fusion–fission cycles. With transitions to agricultural lifeways, building projects directed at collective subsistence infrastructure such as hydraulic projects and terraces created more elaborate anthropogenic landscapes conducive to analysis of resource management and group labor. Importantly, the development of agricultural lifeways in Mesoamerica did not include the domestication of many animal species, and no large ones, with significant implications for available pathways that aspiring elites could pursue in attempts to exert disproportionate control over resources. It also had the effect of creating more common-pool resource strategies in hunted, fished, or collected species. Infrastructure projects such as the Purrón Dam Complex, built by small-scale communities, exceed the scale of others from much larger, state-level societies and should serve as correctives to facile models of labor organization. We can no longer presume that collective production and labor projects require top-down, hierarchical management and must recognize more heterarchical contributions to creating and maintaining public goods. Analyses of monumental constructions must also distinguish, based on architectural and iconographic attributes, whether they were built for inclusive or exclusive purposes.

In a similar vein, models of governance in the deep past should draw from known cases rather than abstract social theory. They should recognize the differing scales of interaction and the fact that more collective intermediate social formations can exist in tension with more exclusionary ones based on patron–client relations; in some places and times the first were relatively more powerful and could push back against elite organization of the second and in others they were weaker and more constrained by unequal social relations. We have queried these issues by exploring shared infrastructure and how it correlates with levels of social inequality and the longevity of urban centers. Finally, when things fell apart and Mesoamerican societies underwent political or demographic declines and societal transformations, we should consider erosion in trust in institutions at least as much as ecological and social stressors, as the two often function relationally. These cases from early Mesoamerica therefore offer varied examples for us to draw on today in managing resources, living in cities, participating in governance, and generally getting along. We return briefly to those in the concluding section.

## 4 Epilogue: What Can We Learn from Early Mesoamerica?

Mesoamerica's deep past provides a varied record of how people survived, changed, and thrived for millennia in diverse environments and through major societal transformations, including adopting and intensifying agriculture, creating interregional networks of trade and interaction, building cities that attracted multiethnic migration, experimenting with a range of governance structures, and persevering through the crimes of colonialism. Mesoamericans invented calendrical systems that were more accurate than what was employed at the time in Europe and developed subsistence regimes and cultural institutions that survived the Spanish invasion and contributed to globalization of the modern era. In general, precolonial Mesoamericans organized themselves in ways that were more equitable than was typical at the time among Eurasian societies, when measured in terms of variables such as Gini scores (Boix 2015; Kohler et al. 2017; Kohler and Smith 2018) and systems of governance (Blanton and Fargher 2008; Carballo 2022; Fargher et al. 2022; Feinman and Nicholas 2020b; Nicholas and Feinman 2022). As a result, there are specific, historical lessons that we can draw from the cases we discuss, but there also are broader, more comparative lessons from this part of the world where we can trace long-term history through time, rather than imposing Eurocentric general models and presumptions from nineteenth- and twentieth-century social theory (Bhambra and Holmwood 2021; Savage 2021). It is therefore in our own interests to not silo the past from the present or the "West from the rest" in public discourse today about topics such as how to avoid resource overexploitation and democratic backsliding and how to foster more equitable and resilient neighborhoods, cities, and polities. Broadening our analytical aperture provides us with the opportunity to assess what worked and what didn't, what was sustainable or not in a wider suite of historical contexts.

History is not inevitable and archaeology provides a temporally deep and materially informed lens on past societal formations and human–environment interactions that greatly expands the dataset for analyzing relative successes and failures in collective action. With archaeological cases, we "know" the outcomes even though the causes may not be immediately clear (Grant 2004). Detecting broad patterns within comparative cases is one methodological approach we have advocated for here as well as marshaling the cultural institutions documented historically among Indigenous groups as reasonable parameters for assessing patterning and variability. They provide relevant case studies for initiatives such as the United Nations' Sustainable Development Goals (SDGs), which include fostering more inclusive, participatory, and sustainable cities (SDG 11) as well as just and strong institutions (SDG 16) (UN-Habitat 2020). For the first goal in particular, the United Nations' New Urban Agenda recommends the expansion and protection of public urban spaces; enhancing the livability of urban neighborhoods; fostering more participatory and polycentric governance; and protecting and promoting cultural heritage, including archaeological and historical sites, as a means of strengthening social bonds and ties to place. Comparative analyses of cases from the past that consider issues of space, governance, and ideology, as outlined here, can contribute to working towards all of these critical goals (see also Angelo and Wachsmuth 2020). They demonstrate that humans have successfully pursued multiple pathways to social and ecological resilience based on varied investments in subsistence and urban infrastructure and following varied economic and political regimes, with general trends among the cases in our study supporting propositions that more shared and equitably distributed infrastructure and more inclusive economies and governance led to greater resilience.

In our contemporary, highly industrialized present some of the relationships between resources, governance, and sustainability are bound to diverge from those observed in past contexts. As one example, a comparative analysis of cases that span the spectrum from preindustrial to contemporary industrial societies indicates that those with more inclusive governance initially consume less energy per capita than those with less inclusive governance, but they also grow in population and industrialize faster, likely because of greater trust creating the virtuous cycles needed for more robust economies, and eventually result in greater per capita energy consumption (Freeman et al. 2023). Inclusive governance therefore stimulates demographic growth and affluence, but citizens in industrialized capitalist economies need to advocate and vote

**Figure 26** Photo of *The Embrace* sculpture on Boston Common, a large bronze sculpture based on a photo of an embrace between Martin Luther and Coretta Scott King, by the artist Hank Willis Thomas.

for more sustainable and equitable policies or suffer the result of unregulated industrialism, overconsumption, and heightened wealth disparities.

Addressing today's resource dilemmas and global climate challenges cannot be accomplished through either fully decentralized, local-level management or fully centralized management but instead requires polycentricity, permitting nested scales of decision-making with local-level adaptation and more central institutions operating in tandem (Anderson and Ostrom 2008). We have seen such top-down/bottom-up systems in Mesoamerica in domains such as chinampa and other drain-field systems, coatequitl and other labor-tax structures for public infrastructure projects, and the combined incentivization and regulation of markets. At the level of global climate mitigation today, there is of course no world government to impose top-down policies, and the multiple levels of factionalism among major institutions advocating for or instituting policies – multinational alliances, nongovernmental organizations (NGOs), individual nations' subnational tiers of governance – act in a state of distributed conflict in which incentives may differ at different scales (Aklin and Midlenberger 2020). Operating at a much smaller scale geographically, past societies present analogous cases of confederations and alliances among polities, nonpolitical alliances (e.g., clans, ritual and pilgrimage networks), diversely organized individual polities, and tiers of decision-making factions from paramount rulers to governing councils, noble houses, and non-elite neighborhoods. Contemporary ecological sustainability efforts also benefit by incorporating lessons from traditional ecological knowledge of agricultural practices and land-tenure regimes, such as the sustainable Mesoamerican milpa system and community efforts to promote biodiversity in the region (Barkin 2022).

Lessons from the past and that draw from the traditional knowledge of contemporary Indigenous peoples are critical to broaden our perspective on what norms and institutions succeeded or failed within various settings at sustainability in managing fisheries, forests, and water resources and governing what remaining commons we have (Ostrom 1990, 2009). Returning to the historical common where we started, Boston Common, we can contemplate the symbolic significance of a much newer bronze artifact inaugurated just recently, in 2023, an aspirational work of public art in a city with a tortured racial history (Figure 26). *The Embrace* sculpture, created by Hank Willis Thomas, was inspired by a photograph of Martin Luther King Jr. and Coretta Scott King, who met in Boston, embracing after learning that King Jr. was being awarded the Nobel Prize for his work on social and racial justice. It is situated near the bandstand from which King addressed a crowd of 22,000 people gathered in the Common who had marched from the predominantly Black neighborhood of Roxbury on April 23, 1965 (Sharif 2012). Without targeting Boston specifically, King's speech that day alluded to issues of de facto segregation in housing and schooling that would erupt in racialized violence within Boston a decade later. Of his creation, Willis Thomas writes: "By highlighting the act of embrace, this sculpture shifts the emphasis from a singular hero worship to collective action, imploring those curious enough to investigate closer. Located at a crossroads in the Common, the landscape around the memorial reinforces the need for collective action inspired by love."[1]

In its initial incarnation, use of Boston Common as a common-pool resource for grazing animals was restricted to adult white males, and *The Embrace* clearly represents progress towards broader inclusion and enfranchisement made in the centuries since then yet also democratic ideals that are still only partially realized today. Dr. King's speech on the Common took place in between the signing into law of the Voting Rights Act and the violence in Selma, Alabama, that he and other civil rights marchers faced in fighting for democratic representation. Heather McGhee (2021: 158) observes how this violence and voter suppression are grounded in a "zero-sum vision of

---

[1] "*The Embrace*, Boston Common Permanent Monument," Hank Willis Thomas (website), (accessed May 6, 2023).

democracy," one that imagines that greater enfranchisement erodes the power of those who already wield it without considering collective gains that come from solidarity among all factions through fully realizing ideals of democratic governance.

Today's autocrats and power factions looking to undermine democratic governance through exclusion do so by fostering vicious cycles of distrust in the keystone institutions that support it (Levi 2022). The erosion of trust in our institutions of governance, education, science, and health creates social stressors that leave us vulnerable to broader ecological stressors – environmental, disease – in ways that operate at different scales and levels of global interconnectivity than past contexts but share some analogs with historical cases of collapse, reconfiguration, and resilience. We can learn from early Mesoamericans and other comparative cases how community participation in shared labor and infrastructure creates virtuous cycles of trust and social capital (Onyx and Bullen 2000) and how more inclusive systems can pay social dividends by widening the pool of willing participants in civic life (McGhee 2021). An understanding of the ways in which people have succeeded and failed at working cooperatively and collectively towards shared goals, informed by a deep-time, comparative perspective, both creates a fuller picture of human history and widens the scope of possible solutions to our pressing concerns of today.

# References

Acemoglu, Daron, and James A. Robinson (2012) *Why Nations Fail: The Origins of Power, Prosperity, and Poverty.* New York: Crown.

Acheson, James M. (2011) Ostrom for Anthropologists. *International Journal of the Commons* 5(2), 319–339.

(2015) Private Land and Common Oceans: Analysis of the Development of Property Regimes. *Current Anthropology* 56(1), 28–55.

Aklin, Michaël, and Matto Mildenberger (2020) Prisoners of the Wrong Dilemma: Why Distributive Conflict, Not Collective Action, Characterizes the Politics of Climate Change. *Global Environmental Politics* 20(4), 4–26.

Alcántara Gallegos, Alejandro (2004) Los barrios de Tenochtitlan: topografía, organización interna y tipología de sus predios. In *Historia de la vida cotidiana en M'exico, Tomo I, Mesoamérica y los ámbitos indígenas de la Nueva España*, edited by Pablo Escalante Gonzalbo, pp. 167–198. Mexico City: El Colegio de México, Fondo de Cultura Económica.

Andersson, Krister P., and Elinor Ostrom (2008) Analyzing Decentralized Resource Regimes from a Polycentric Perspective. *Policy Sciences* 41(1), 71–93.

Angelo, Hillary, and David Wachsmuth (2020) Why Does Everyone Think Cities Can Save the Planet? *Urban Studies* 57(11), 2201–2221.

Arroyo Abad, Leticia, and Noel Maurer Jr. (2021) History Never Really Says Goodbye: A Critical Review of Persistence Literature. *Journal of Historical Political Economy* 1(1), 31–68, http://dx.doi.org/10.1561/115.00000002.

Ashmore, Wendy (1984) Classic Maya Wells at Quirigua, Guatemala: Household Facilities in a Water-Rich Setting. *American Antiquity* 49(1), 147–153.

Aveni, Anthony F. (2005) Observations on the Pecked Designs and other Figures Carved on the South Platform of the Pyramid of the Sun at Teotihuacan. *Journal for the History of Astronomy* 36(122), 31–47.

Aveni, Anthony F., Iain Morley, and Colin Renfrew (2010) The Measure of Time in Mesoamerica: From Teotihuacan to the Maya. In *The Archaeology of Measurement: Comprehending Heaven, Earth and Time in Ancient Societies*, edited by Iain Morley and Colin Renfrew, pp. 203–215. New York: Cambridge University Press.

Bagley, Joseph M. (2016) *A History of Boston in 50 Artifacts.* Hanover: University Press of New England.

Banning, Edward Bruce, and Gary Graham Coupland (eds.) (1996) *People Who Lived in Big Houses: Archaeological Perspectives on Large Domestic Structures*. Madison, WI: Prehistory Press.

Barkin, David (2022) Shaping a Communitarian Ethos in an Era of Ecological Crisis. *Frontiers in Sustainability* 3, 944252, https://doi.org/10.3389/frsus.2022.944252.

Barua, Maan (2021) Infrastructure and Non-human Life: A Wider Ontology. *Progress in Human Geography* 45(6), 1467–1489.

Bateson, Gregory (1935) Culture Contact and Schismogenesis. *Man* 35, 178–183.

(1936) *Naven: A Survey of the Problems Suggested by a Composite Picture of the Culture of a New Guinea Tribe Drawn from Three Points of View*. Cambridge: Cambridge University Press.

Bayman, James M., and Alan P. Sullivan III (2008) Property, Identity, and Macroeconomy in the Prehispanic Southwest. *American Anthropologist* 110(1), 6–20.

Beach, Timothy, Sheryl Luzzadder-Beach, Samantha Krause et al. (2019) Ancient Maya Wetland Fields Revealed under Tropical Forest Canopy from Laser Scanning and Multiproxy Evidence. *Proceedings of the National Academy of Sciences* 116(43), 21469–21477.

Berdan, Frances E. (2014) *Aztec Archaeology and Ethnohistory*. New York: Cambridge University Press.

Bhambra, Gurminder K., and John Holmwood (2021) *Colonialism and Modern Social Theory*. Cambridge: Polity Press.

Birch, Jennifer (2022) Premodern Confederacies: Balancing Strategic Collective Action and Local Autonomy. *Frontiers in Political Science* 4, 807239, https://doi.org/10.3389/fpos.2022.807239.

Birkett, Brooke A., Jonathan Obrist-Farner, Prudence M. Rice et al. (2023) Preclassic Environmental Degradation of Lake Petén Itzá, Guatemala, by the Early Maya of Nixtun-Ch'ich'. *Nature Communications: Earth and Environment* 4(1), https://doi.org/10.1038/s43247-023-00726-4.

Blanton, Richard E. (1994) *Houses and Households: A Comparative Study*. New York: Springer.

(2013) Cooperation and the Moral Economy of the Marketplace. In *Merchants, Markets, and Exchange in the Pre-Columbian World*, edited by Kenneth G. Hirth and Joanne Pillsbury, pp. 23–48. Washington, DC: Dumbarton Oaks and Trustees of Harvard University.

(2015) Theories of Ethnicity and the Dynamics of Ethnic Change in Multiethnic Societies. *Proceedings of the National Academy of Sciences* 112(30), 9176–9181.

Blanton, Richard E., and Lane Fargher (2008) *Collective Action and the Formation of Pre-modern States*. New York: Springer.

(2011) The Collective Logic of Pre-modern Cities. *World Archaeology* 43(3), 505–522.

(2012) Market Cooperation and the Evolution of the Pre-Hispanic Mesoamerican World System. In *Routledge Handbook of World-Systems Analysis*, edited by Salvatore J. Babones and Christopher Chase-Dunn, pp. 11–20. London: Routledge.

(2016) *How Humans Cooperate: Confronting the Challenges of Collective Action*. Boulder: University Press of Colorado.

Blanton, Richard E., Lane F. Fargher, and Verenice Y. Heredia Espinoza (2005) The Mesoamerican World of Goods and Its Transformations. In *Settlement, Subsistence, and Social Complexity: Essays Honoring the Legacy of Jeffrey R. Parsons*, edited by Richard E. Blanton, pp. 260–294. Los Angeles, CA: Cotsen Institute of Archaeology.

Blanton, Richard E., Gary M. Feinman, Stephen A. Kowalewski, and Linda M. Nicholas (2022) *Ancient Oaxaca: The Monte Albán State*. 2nd ed. New York: Cambridge University Press.

Boehm, Christopher (2012) *Moral Origins: The Evolution of Virtue, Altruism, and Shame*. New York: Basic.

Boix, Carles (2015) *Political Order and Inequality: Their Foundations and Their Consequences for Human Welfare*. New York: Cambridge University Press.

Bowles, Samuel, and Herbert Gintis (2002) Social Capital and Community Governance. *The Economic Journal* 112(483), 419–436.

Brumfiel, Elizabeth M. (2011) Technologies of Time: Calendrics and Commoners in Postclassic Mexico. *Ancient Mesoamerica* 22, 53–70.

Byers, Douglas S. (1962) The Restoration and Preservation of Some Objects from Etowah. *American Antiquity* 28(2), 206–216.

Cabrera Castro, Rubén, and Sergio Gómez Chávez (2008) La Ventilla: A Model for a Barrio in the Urban Structure of Teotihuacan. In *Urbanism in Mesoamerica*, Vol. 2, edited by Alba Guadalupe Mastache, Robert H. Cobean, Ángel García Cook, and Kenneth G. Hirth, pp. 37–84. University Park, PA: Instituto Nacional de Antropología e Historia and Pennsylvania State University.

Carballo, David M. (2013a) Cultural and Evolutionary Dynamics of Cooperation in Archaeological Perspective. In *Cooperation and Collective Action: Archaeological Perspectives*, edited by David M. Carballo, pp. 3–33. Boulder: University Press of Colorado.

(2013b) Labor Collectives and Group Cooperation in Pre-Hispanic Central Mexico. In *Cooperation and Collective Action: Archaeological*

*Perspectives*, edited by David M. Carballo, pp. 243–274. Boulder: University Press of Colorado.

(ed.) (2013c) *Cooperation and Collective Action: Archaeological Perspectives*. Boulder: University Press of Colorado.

(2016) *Urbanization and Religion in Ancient Central Mexico*. New York: Oxford University Press.

(2020) *Collision of Worlds: A Deep History of the Fall of Aztec Mexico and the Forging of New Spain*. New York: Oxford University Press.

(2022) Governance Strategies in Precolonial Central Mexico. *Frontiers in Political Science* 4, 797331.

Carballo, David M., and Anthony F. Aveni (2012) Los vecinos del Preclásico en Xochitécatl y la institucionalización de la religión. *Arqueología Mexicana* 117, 52–57.

Carballo, David M., Luis Barba, Agustín Ortíz et al. (2021) Excavations at the Southern Neighborhood Center of the Tlajinga District, Teotihuacan, Mexico. *Latin American Antiquity* 32(3), 557–576.

Carballo, David M., and Gary M. Feinman (2016) Cooperation, Collective Action, and the Archaeology of Large-Scale Societies. *Evolutionary Anthropology* 25, 288–296.

Carballo, David M., Gary M. Feinman, and Aurelio López Corral (2022) Mesoamerican Urbanism: Indigenous Institutions, Infrastructure, and Resilience. *Urban Studies*, 00420980221105418, https://doi.org/10.1177/00420980221105418.

Carballo, David M., Paul Roscoe, and Gary M. Feinman (2014) Cooperation and Collective Action in the Cultural Evolution of Complex Societies. *Journal of Archaeological Method and Theory* 21(1), 98–133.

Carrasco, David, Lindsay Jones, and Scott Sessions (eds.) (2000) *Mesoamerica's Classic Heritage: From Teotihuacan to the Aztecs*. Boulder: University Press of Colorado.

Carrasco, Pedro (1971) Social Organization of Ancient Mexico. In *Handbook of Middle American Indians, Vol. 10: Archaeology of Northern Mesoamerica, Part 1*, edited by Gordon F. Ekholm and Ignacio Bernal, pp. 349–375. Austin: University of Texas Press.

(1984) Royal Marriages in Ancient Mexico. In *Explorations in Ethnohistory: Indians of Central Mexico in the Sixteenth Century*, edited by H. R. Harvey and Hanns J. Prem, pp. 41–81. Albuquerque: University of New Mexico Press.

Caso, Alfonso (1966) The Lords of Yanhuitlan. In *Ancient Oaxaca: Discoveries in Mexican Archeology and History*, edited by John Paddock, pp. 313–335. Stanford, CA: Stanford University Press.

Cervantes de Salazar, Francisco (1554/2014) *México en 1554*. Translated by Joaquín García Icazbalceta. Washington, DC: Westphalia Press.

Chwe, Michael Suk-Young (2001) *Rational Ritual: Culture, Coordination, and Common Knowledge*. Princeton, NJ: Princeton University Press.

Clark, John E., and John G. Hodgson (2021) Wetland Villages in Soconusco, 6000–2000 BCE: A New Interpretation of Archaic Shell Mounds. In *Preceramic Mesoamerica*, edited by Jon C. Lohse, Aleksander Borejsza, and Arthur A. Joyce, pp 420–447. New York: Routledge.

Coe, Michael D., and Richard A. Diehl (1980) *In the Land of the Olmec, Vol. 1: The Archaeology of San Lorenzo Tenochtitlán*. Austin: University of Texas Press.

Cohen, Jeffrey H. (1999) *Cooperation and Community: Economy and Society in Oaxaca*. Austin: University of Texas Press.

Cordova, Carlos E. (2022) *The Lakes of the Basin of Mexico: Dynamics of a Lacustrine System and the Evolution of a Civilization*. New York: Springer.

Cordova, Carlos E., Luis Morett-Alatorre, Charles Frederick, and Lorena Gámez-Eternod (2022) Lacustrine Dynamics and Tlatel-Type Settlements from Middle Formative to Late Aztec in the Eastern Part of Lake Texcoco, Mexico. *Ancient Mesoamerica* 33(2), 211–226.

Cortés, Hernán (1986) *Letters from Mexico*. Edited and translated by Anthony Pagden. New Haven, CT: Yale University Press.

Crassard, Rémy, Wael Abu-Azizeh, Olivier Barge et al. (2022) The Use of Desert Kites as Hunting Mega-Traps: Functional Evidence and Potential Impacts on Socioeconomic and Ecological Spheres. *Journal of World Prehistory* 35(1), 1–44.

Crassard, Rémy, Wael Abu-Azizeh, Olivier Barge et al. (2023) The Oldest Plans to Scale of Humanmade Mega-Structures. *PLoS ONE* 18(5): e0277927, https://doi.org/10.1371/journal.pone.0277927.

Creamer, Winifred (1987) Mesoamerica as a Concept: An Archaeological View from Central America. *Latin American Research Review* 22(1), 35–62.

Cyphers, Ann, and Anna Di Castro (2009) Early Olmec Architecture and Imagery. In *The Art of Urbanism: How Mesoamerican Kingdoms Represented Themselves in Architecture and Imagery*, edited by William L. Fash and Leonardo López Luján, pp. 21–52. Washington, DC: Dumbarton Oaks Research Library and Collections, Harvard University Press.

D'Altroy, Terrance, and Timothy K. Earle (1985) Staple Finance, Wealth Finance, and Storage in the Inka Political Economy. *Current Anthropology* 26, 187–206.

Dickens, Roy S., Jr., and James McKinley (2003) *Frontiers in the Soil: The Archaeology of Georgia*. 2nd ed. Atlanta: The Society for Georgia Archaeology.

Doolittle, William E. (1990) *Canal Irrigation in Prehistoric Mexico: The Sequence of Technological Change.* Austin: University of Texas Press.

Dungan, Katherine A., and Matthew A. Peeples (2018) Public Architecture as Performance Space in the Prehispanic Central Southwest. *Journal of Anthropological Archaeology* 50, 12–26.

Eberl, Markus, Sven Gronemeyer, and Claudia Marie Vela González (2023) The Early Classic Genesis of the Royal Maya Capital of Tamarindito. *Latin American Antiquity* 34(1), 40–58.

Eerkens, Jelmer W. (1999) Common Pool Resources, Buffer Zones, and Jointly Owned Territories: Hunter-Gatherer Land and Resource Tenure in Fort Irwin, Southeastern California. *Human Ecology* 27, 297–318.

Evans, Susan Toby (2005) Men, Women, and Maguey: The Household Division of Labor among Aztec Farmers. In *Settlement, Subsistence, and Social Complexity: Essays Honoring the Legacy of Jeffrey R. Parsons*, edited by Richard E. Blandon, pp. 198–228. Los Angeles: Cotsen Institute of Archaeology, University of California – Los Angeles.

Evans, Susan Toby, and Deborah L. Nichols (2015) Water Temples and Civil Engineering at Teotihuacan, Mexico. In *Human Adaptation in Ancient Mesoamerica*, edited by Nancy Gonlin and Kirk D. French, pp. 25–51. Boulder: University Press of Colorado.

Fargher, Lane F. (2016) Corporate Power Strategies, Collective Action, and Control of Principals: A Cross-Cultural Approach. In *Alternate Pathways to Complexity*, edited by Lane F. Fargher and Verenice Y. Heredia Espinoza, pp. 309–326. Boulder: University Press of Colorado.

Fargher, Lane F., Richard E. Blanton, and Verenice Y. Heredia Espinoza (2010) Egalitarian Ideology and Political Power in Prehispanic Central Mexico: The Case of Tlaxcallan. *Latin American Antiquity* 21(3), 227–251.

(2017) Aztec State-Making, Politics, and Empires: The Triple Alliance. In *The Oxford Handbook of the Aztecs*, edited by Deborah L. Nichols and Enrique Rodríguez-Alegría, pp. 143–160. New York: Oxford University Press.

(2022) Collective Action, Good Government, and Democracy in Tlaxcallan, Mexico: An Analysis Based on Demokratia. *Frontiers in Political Science* 4, 832440.

Fargher, Lane F., Richard E. Blanton, Verenice Y. Heredia Espinoza et al. (2011) Tlaxcallan: The Archaeology of an Ancient Republic in the New World. *Antiquity* 85(327), 172–186.

Fairbanks, Charles H. (1946) The Macon Earth Lodge. *American Antiquity* 12(2), 94–108.

Fash, William L. (2001) *Scribes, Warriors and Kings: The City of Copán and the Ancient Maya*. Revised ed. New York: Thames and Hudson.

Fedick, Scott L., Shanti Morell-Hart, and Lydie Dussol (2023) Agriculture in the Ancient Maya Lowlands (Part 2): Landesque Capital and Long-Term Resource Management Strategies. *Journal of Archaeological Research*, https://doi.org/10.1007/s10814-023-09185-z.

Feinman, Gary M. (2016) Variation and Change in Archaic States: Ritual as a Mechanism of Sociopolitical Integration. In *Ritual and Archaic States*, edited by Joanne M. A. Murphy, pp. 1–22. Gainesville: University Press of Florida.

(2022) Reframing Historical Rhymes from the Dawn of Everything. *Ciodynamics*, https://doi.org/10.21237/C7clio0057267.

Feinman, Gary M., and David M. Carballo (2018) Collaborative and Competitive Strategies in the Variability and Resiliency of Large-Scale Societies in Mesoamerica. *Economic Anthropology* 5(1), 7–19.

(2022) Communication, Computation, and Governance: A Multiscalar Vantage on the Prehispanic Mesoamerican World. *Journal of Social Computing* 3(1), 91–118.

Feinman, Gary M., David M. Carballo, Linda M. Nicholas, and Stephen A. Kowalewski (2023) Sustainability and Duration of Early Central Places in Prehispanic Mesoamerica. *Frontiers in Ecology and Evolution* 11, https://doi.org/10.3389/fevo.2023.1076740.

Feinman, Gary M., Ronald K. Faulseit, and Linda M. Nicholas (2018) Assessing Wealth Inequality in the Pre-Hispanic Valley of Oaxaca: Comparative Implications. In *Ten Thousand Years of Inequality: The Archaeology of Wealth Differences*, edited by Timothy A. Kohler and Michael E. Smith, pp. 262–287. Tucson: University of Arizona Press.

Feinman, Gary M., and Jill E. Neitzel (2023) The Social Dynamics of Settling Down. *Journal of Anthropological Archaeology* 69: 101468.

Feinman, Gary M., and Linda M. Nicholas (2016) Reconsiderando la "invasión mixteca" del valle de Oaxaca en el Posclásico. *Anales de Antropología* 50, 247–265.

(2020a) Teotihuacan and Oaxaca: Assessing Prehispanic Relations. In *Teotihuacan: The World beyond the City*, edited by Kenneth G. Hirth, David M. Carballo, and Barbara Arroyo, pp. 331–369. Washington, DC: Dumbarton Oaks and Trustees for Harvard University.

(2020b) Framing Inequality in Ancient Civilizations. In *Poverty and Inequality in Early Civilizations*, edited by Richard Bussmann and Tobias Helms, pp. 107–117. Bonn: Habelt-Verlag.

Feinman, Gary M., Linda M. Nicholas, and Mark Golitko (2022) Macroscale Shifts in Obsidian Procurement Networks across Prehispanic Mesoamerica. In *Obsidian across the Americas: Compositional Studies Conducted in the Elemental Analysis Facility at the Field Museum of Natural History*, edited by Gary M. Feinman and Danielle J. Riebe, pp. 98–123. Oxford: Archaeopress.

Fisher, Kevin D. (2009) Placing Social Interaction: An Integrative Approach to Analyzing Past Built Environments. *Journal of Anthropological Archaeology* 28, 439–457.

Flor, Jan L. (1998) Social Capital and Communities of Place. *Rural Sociology* 63(4), 481–506.

Florescano, Enrique (2017) The Creation, Rise, and Decline of Mexica Power. In *The Oxford Handbook of the Aztecs*, edited by Deborah L. Nichols and Enrique Rodríguez-Alegría, pp. 93–106. New York: Oxford University Press.

Foias, Antonia E. (2013) *Ancient Maya Political Dynamics*. Gainesville: University Press of Florida.

Fowler, Melvin L. (1987) Early Water Management at Amalucan, State of Puebla, Mexico. *National Geographic Research* 3, 52–68.

Frederick Charles D. (2007) Chinampa Cultivation in the Basin of Mexico. In *Seeking a Richer Harvest*, edited by Tina L. Thurston and T. Christopher Fisher, pp. 107–124. New York: Springer.

Freeman, Jacob, Jacopo A. Baggio, Lux Miranda, and John M. Anderies (2023) Infrastructure and the Energy Use of Human Polities. *Cross-Cultural Research* 57(2–3), 294–322, https://doi.org/10.1177/1069397122114977.

Gándara, Manuel (2012) A Short History of Theory in Mesoamerican Archaeology. In *The Oxford Handbook of Mesoamerican Archaeology*, edited by Deborah L. Nichols and Christopher A. Pool, pp. 31–46. New York: Oxford University Press.

Gillespie, Susan D. (1989) *The Aztec Kings: The Construction of Rulership in Mexica History*. Tucson: University of Arizona Press.

Glowacki, Luke (2020) The Emergence of Locally Adaptive Institutions: Insights from Traditional Social Structures of East African Pastoralists. *BioSystems* 198, 104257.

Golden, Charles, and Andrew K. Scherer (2013) Territory, Trust, Growth, and Collapse in Classic Period Maya kingdoms. *Current Anthropology* 54(4), 397–435.

Gómez Chávez, Sergio (2022) Los barrios y sus componentes en Teotihuacan. Un modelo de barrio y su articulación urbana. In *Estudios de un barrio de la antigua ciudad de Teotihuacan: Memorias del Proyecto La Ventilla 1992–2004*, Vol. 2, edited by Rubén Cabrera Castro and Serio Gómez Chávez, pp. 11–82. Mexico City: Instituto Nacional de Antropología e Historia.

Good, Catharine (2005) Ejes conceptuales entre los Nahuas de Guerrero: expresión de un modelo fenomenológico mesoamericano. *Estudios de cultura náhuatl* 36, 87–113.

Graeber, David, and David Wengrow (2021) *The Dawn of Everything: A New History of Humanity.* New York: Farrar, Straus and Giroux.

Grant, Jill (2004) Sustainable Urbanism in Historical Perspective. In *Towards Sustainable Cities: East Asian, North American, and European Perspectives on Managing Urban Regions*, edited by André Sorensen, Peter J. Marcutullio, and Jill Grant, pp. 24–37. Burlington, VT: Ashgate.

Green, Adam S. (2022) Of Revenue Without Rulers: Public Goods in the Egalitarian Cities of the Indus Civilization. *Frontiers in Political Science* 4, 823071.

Gutiérrez Mendoza, Gerardo (2012) Hacia un modelo general para entender la estructura político-territorial del Estado nativo mesoamericano (*altepetl*). In *El poder compartido: ensayos sobre la arqueología de organizaciones políticas segmentarias y oligárquicas*, edited by Annick Daneels and Gerardo Gutiérrez Mendoza, pp. 27–67. Mexico City: Centro de Investigaciones y Estudios Superiores en Antropología Social and El Colegio de Michoacán.

Hajovsky, Patrick Thomas (2015) *On the Lips of Others: Moteuczoma's Fame in Aztec Monuments and Rituals.* Austin: University of Texas Press.

Hansen, Richard D., Carlos Morales-Aguilar, Josephine Thompson et al. (2022) LiDAR Analyses in the Contiguous Mirador-Calakmul Karst Basin, Guatemala: An Introduction to New Perspectives on Regional Early Maya Socioeconomic and Political Organization. *Ancient Mesoamerica*, https://doi.org/10.1017/S0956536122000244.

Hardin, Garrett (1968) The Tragedy of the Commons. *Science* 162(3859), 1243–1248.

(1998) Extensions of "The Tragedy of the Commons." *Science* 280(5364), 682–683.

Hardin, Russell (2003) Gaming Trust. In *Trust and Reciprocity: Interdisciplinary Lessons from Experimental Research*, edited by Elinor Ostrom and James Walker, pp. 80–101. New York: Russell Sage Foundation.

Harrison, Hannah L., and Philip A. Loring (2014) Larger Than Life: The Emergent Nature of Conflict in Alaska's Upper Cook Inlet Salmon Fisheries. *SAGE Open* (4), 1–14.

Harvey, H. R. (1984) Aspects of Land Tenure in Ancient Mexico. In *Explorations in Ethnohistory: Indians of Central Mexico in the Sixteenth Century*, edited by H. R. Harvey and Hanns J. Prem, pp. 83–102. Albuquerque: University of New Mexico Press.

Hassig, Ross (2016) *Polygamy and the Rise and Demise of the Aztec Empire*. Albuquerque: University of New Mexico Press.

Helmke, Christophe, and Jesper Nielsen (2021) Teotihuacan Writing: Where Are We Now? *Visible Language* 55(2), 29–73.

Henderson, Hope (2003) The Organization of Staple Crop Production at K'axob, Belize. *Latin American Antiquity* 14(4), 469–496.

Hicks, Frederic (1984) Rotational Labor and Urban Development in Prehispanic Tetzcoco. In *Explorations in Ethnohistory: Indians of Central Mexico in the Sixteenth Century*, edited by H. R. Harvey and Hanns, J. Prem, pp. 147–174. Albuquerque, University of New Mexico Press.

(1999) The Middle Class in Ancient Central Mexico. *Journal of Anthropological Research* 55(3), 409–427.

Hirth, Kenneth G. (2016) *The Aztec Economic World: Merchants and Markets in Ancient Mesoamerica*. New York: Cambridge University Press.

(2020) *The Organization of Ancient Economies: A Global Perspective*. New York: Cambridge University Press.

Hoggarth, Julie A., Matthew Restall, James W. Wood, and Douglas J. Kennett (2017) Drought and Its Demographic Effects in the Maya Lowlands. *Current Anthropology* 58(1), 82–113.

Holland-Lulewicz, Jacob, Victor D. Thompson, Jennifer Birch, and Colin Grier (2022) Keystone Institutions of Democratic Governance across Indigenous North America. *Frontiers in Political Science* 4, 840049.

Hutson, Scott R. (2016) *The Ancient Urban Maya: Neighborhoods, Inequality, and Built Form*. Gainesville: University Press of Florida.

Hutson, Scott R., Nicholas P. Dunning, Bruce Cook et al. (2021) Ancient Maya Rural Settlement Patterns, Household Cooperation, and Regional Subsistence Interdependency in the Río Bec Area: Contributions from G-LiHT. *Journal of Anthropological Research* 77(4), 550–579.

Inomata, Takeshi (2006) Plazas, Performers, and Spectators: Political Theaters of the Classic Maya. *Current Anthropology* 47(5), 805–842.

Inomata, Takeshi, Daniela Triadan, Verónica A. Vázquez López et al. (2020) Monumental Architecture at Aguada Fénix and the Rise of Maya Civilization. *Nature* 582(7813), 530–533.

Jansen, Maarten E., and Gabina Aurora Pérez Jiménez (2011) *The Mixtec Pictorial Manuscripts: Time, Agency and Memory in Ancient Mexico*. Leiden: Brill.

Jensen Jeffrey L., and Adam J. Ramey (2020) Early Investments in State Capacity Promote Persistently Higher Levels of Social Capital. *Proceedings of the National Academy of Sciences* 117(20), 10755–10761.

Joyce, Rosemary A. (2021) Mesoamerica: From Culture Area to Networks of Communities of Practice. In *Mesoamerican Archaeology: Theory and Practice*, edited by Julia A. Hendon, Lisa Overholtzer, and Rosemary A. Joyce, pp. 1–31. Hoboken, NJ: John Wiley & Sons.

Kaufman, Terrance, and John Justeson (2009) Historical Linguistics and Pre-Columbian Mesoamerica. *Ancient Mesoamerica* 20, 221–231.

Kelly, Arthur Randolph (1938) *A Preliminary Report on Archeological Explorations at Macon, Ga.* Bureau of American Ethnology Bulletin 119. Washington, DC: Smithsonian Institution.

Kirchhoff, Paul (1943) Mesoamérica: sus límites geográficos, composición étnica y caracteres culturales. *Acta Americana* 1, 92–107.

Klinenberg, Eric (2018) *Palaces for the People: How Social Infrastructure Can Help Fight Inequality, Polarization, and the Decline of Civic Life.* New York: Crown.

Kohler, Timothy A. (1992) Field Houses, Villages, and the Tragedy of the Commons in the Early Northern Anasazi Southwest. *American Antiquity* 57(4), 617–635.

Kohler, Timothy A., and Michael E. Smith (eds.) (2018) *Ten Thousand Years of Inequality: The Archaeology of Wealth Differences.* Tucson: University of Arizona Press.

Kohler, Timothy A., Michael E. Smith, Amy Bogaard et al. (2017) Greater Post-Neolithic Wealth Disparities in Eurasia Than in North America and Mesoamerica. *Nature* 551(7694), 619–622.

Kowalewski Stephen A., Gary M. Feinman, Linda M. Nichols, and Verenice Y. Heredia (2006) Hilltowns and Valley Fields: Great Transformations, Labor, and Long-Term History in Ancient Oaxaca. In *Labor in Cross-Cultural Perspective*, edited by E. Paul Durrenberger and Judith Martí, pp. 197–216. Lanham, MD: AltaMira Press.

Kowalewski, Stephen A., and Verenice Y. Heredia Espinoza (2020) Mesoamerica as an Assemblage of Institutions. In *The Evolution of Social Institutions: Interdisciplinary Perspectives*, Dimitri M. Bondarenko, Stephen A. Kowalewski, and David B. Small (eds.), pp. 495–522. New York: Springer.

Latham, Alan, and Jack Layton (2019) Social Infrastructure and the Public Life of Cities: Studying Urban Sociality and Public spaces. *Geography Compass* 13(7), e12444.

Leach, Edmund R. (1954) *Political Systems of Highland of Highland Burma: A Study of Kachin Social Structure.* 1st ed. London: G. Bell & Son.

(1977) *Political Systems of Highland Burma: A Study of Kachin Social Structure.* Reprinted ed. Atlantic Highlands, NJ: The Athlone Press.

Lentz, David L., Nicholas P. Dunning, and Vernon L. Scarborough (eds.) (2015) *Tikal: Paleoecology of an Ancient Maya City.* New York: Cambridge University Press.

Lentz, David, Nicholas Dunning, Payson Sheets et al. (2022) Ancient Maya Intensive Agriculture and Water Management Practices. In *Sustainability and Water Management in the Maya World and Beyond*, edited by Jean T. Larmon, Lisa J. Lucero, and Fred Valdez Jr., pp. 52–77. Boulder: University Press of Colorado.

León-Portilla, Miguel (ed.) (1991) *Huehuehtlahtolli: Testimonios de la antiqua palabra.* Mexico City: Fondo de Cultura Económica.

Levi, Margaret (1988) *Of Rule and Revenue.* Berkeley: University of California Press.

(1996) *A State of Trust.* European University Institute (EUI) Working Paper RSC No. 96/23. San Domenico: Badia Fiesolana.

(2022) Trustworthy Government: The Obligations of Government and the Responsibilities of the Governed. *Daedalus* 141(4), 241–259.

Lewis, Oscar (1963) *Life in a Mexican Village: Tepoztlán Restudied.* Urbana: University of Illinois Press.

Lind, Michael (2012) La estructura político-territorial del altépetl de Cholula. In *El poder compartido: ensayos sobre la arqueología de organizaciones políticas segmentarias y oligárquicas*, edited by Annick Daneels and Gerardo Gutiérrez Mendoza, pp. 99–113. Mexico City: Centro de Investigaciones y Estudios Superiores en Antropología Social and El Colegio de Michoacán.

Lloyd, William Forester (1833) *Two Lectures on the Checks to Population.* Oxford: Oxford University Press.

Lockhart, James (1992) *The Nahuas after the Conquest: A Social and Cultural History of the Indians of Central Mexico, Sixteenth through Eighteenth Centuries.* Stanford, CA: Stanford University Press.

(1993) *We People Here: Nahuatl Accounts of the Conquest of Mexico.* Berkeley: University of California Press.

López Austin, Alfredo (1961) *La Constitución Real de México-Tenochtitlan.* Mexico City: Universidad Nacional Autónoma de México.

López Corral, Aurelio (2023) When Tlaxcalteca Met Olmeca Xicallanca: Epiclassic to Early Postclassic Chronology and Cultural Change in the Puebla-Tlaxcala Region. In *When East Meets West: Chichén Itza, Tula, and the Postclassic Mesoamerican World*, Vol. 2, edited by Travis W. Stanton, Karl A. Taube, Jeremy D. Coltman, and Nelda I. Marengo Camacho, pp. 525–536. Oxford: BAR Publishing.

Luna Golya, Gregory G. (2014) Modeling the Aztec Agricultural Waterscape of Lake Xochimilco: A GIS Analysis of Lakebed Chinampas and Settlement. Unpublished PhD dissertation, The Pennsylvania State University.

Lyman, R. Lee, and Michael J. O'Brien. (2001) The Direct Historical Approach, Analogical Reasoning, and Theory in Americanist Archaeology. *Journal of Archaeological Method and Theory* 8, 303–342.

Manzanilla, Linda R. (2015) Cooperation and Tensions in Multiethnic Corporate Societies Using Teotihuacan, Central Mexico, as a Case Study. *Proceedings of the National Academy of Sciences* 112(30), 9210–9215.

(2017) Teopancazco: A Multiethnic Neighborhood Center in the Metropolis of Teotihuacan. In *Multiethnicity and Migration at Teopancazco: Investigations of a Teotihuacan Neighborhood Center*, edited by Linda R. Manzanilla, pp. 1–48. Gainesville: University Press of Florida.

Marcus, Joyce (1992) *Mesoamerican Writing Systems: Propaganda, Myth, and History in Four Ancient Civilizations*. Princeton, NJ: Princeton University Press.

Marcus, Joyce, and Kent V. Flannery (1996) *Zapotec Civilization: How Urban Society Evolved in Mexico's Oaxaca Valley*. New York: Thames and Hudson.

Martin, Simon (2020) *Ancient Maya Politics: A Political Anthropology of the Classic Period 150–900 CE*. New York: Cambridge University Press.

Martínez Gracida, Araceli Rojas (2017) El agua en el cerro del Rayo: nueva evidencia sobre la presencia y manejo del agua en Monte Albán. *Revista Española de Antropología Americana* 47, 15–42.

Masson, Marilyn, and Carlos Peraza Lope (eds.) (2014) *Kukulcan's Realm: Urban Life at Ancient Mayapán*. Boulder: University Press of Colorado.

McGhee, Heather (2021) *The Sum of Us: What Racism Costs Everyone and How We Can Prosper Together*. New York: One World.

Melis, Alicia P., and Dirk Semmann (2010) How Is Human Cooperation Different? *Philosophical Transactions of the Royal Society B* 365, 2663–2674.

Mildenberger, Matto (2019) The Tragedy of the Tragedy of the Commons. *Scientific American*, April 23, https://blogs.scientificamerican.com/voices/the-tragedy-of-the-tragedy-of-the-commons/.

Millhauser, John K. (2017) Aztec Use of Lake Resources in the Basin of Mexico. In *The Oxford Handbook of the Aztecs*, edited by Deborah L. Nichols and Enrique Rodríguez-Alegría, pp. 301–318. New York: Oxford University Press.

Millhauser, John K., and Lisa Overholtzer (2020) Commodity Chains in Archaeological Research: Cotton Cloth in the Aztec Economy. *Journal of Archaeological Research* 28, 187–240.

Molina, Fray Alonso de (2008) *Vocabulario en lengua castellana y mexicana.* 6th ed. Mexico City: Editorial Porrúa.

Monaghan, John (1990) Reciprocity, Redistribution, and the Transaction of Value in the Mesoamerican Fiesta. *American Ethnologist* 17(4), 758–774.

(1996) Fiesta Finance in Mesoamerica and the Origins of Gift Exchange Systems. *Journal of the Royal Anthropological Institute* 2, 499–516.

Morehart, Christopher (2017) Aztec Agricultural Strategies: Intensification, Landesque Capital, and the Sociopolitics of Production. In *The Oxford Handbook of the Aztecs*, edited by Deborah L. Nichols and Enrique Rodríguez-Alegría, pp. 263–279. New York: Oxford University Press.

(2018) The Political Ecology of Chinampa Landscapes in the Basin of Mexico. In *Water and Power in Ancient Societies*, edited by Emily Holt, pp. 19–39. The Institute for European and Mediterranean Archaeology Distinguished Monograph Series. Buffalo: State University of New York.

Murakami, Tatsuya (2015) Replicative Construction Experiments at Teotihuacan, Mexico: Assessing the Duration and Timing of Monumental Construction. *Journal of Field Archaeology* 40(3), 263–282.

Neely, James A., Michael J. Aiuvalasit, and Vincent A. Clause (2015) New Light on the Prehistoric Purrón Dam Complex: Small Corporate Group Collaboration in the Tehuacán Valley, Puebla, México. *Journal of Field Archaeology* 40(3), 347–364.

Neely, James A., Michael J. Aiuvalasit, and Barbara M. Winsborough (2022) Relict Canals of the Tehuacán Valley, Mexico: A Middle- to Late-Holocene Dryland Socio-Hydrological System. *The Holocene* 32(12), 1422–1436.

Nicholas, Linda M., and Gary M. Feinman (2022) The Foundation of Monte Albán, Intensification, and Growth: Coactive Processes and Joint Production. *Frontiers in Political Science* 4, 805047.

Nichols, Deborah L., Frances F. Berdan, and Michael E. Smith (eds.) (2017) *Rethinking the Aztec Economy.* Tucson: University of Arizona Press.

Nichols, Deborah L., Charles D. Frederick, Luis Morett Alatorre, and Fernando Sánchez Martínez (2006) Water Management and Political Economy in Formative Period Central Mexico. In *Precolumbian Water Management: Ideology, Ritual, and Power*, edited by Lisa J. Lucero and Barbara W. Fash, pp. 51–66. Tucson: University of Arizona Press.

Nugent, David (1982) Closed Systems and Contradiction: The Kachin in and out of History. *Man* 17(3), 508–527.

O'Brien, Michael J., Dennis E. Lewarch, Roger D. Mason, and James A. Neely (1980) Functional Analysis of Water Control Features at Monte Alban, Oaxaca, Mexico. *World Archaeology* 11(3), 342–355.

Offner, Jerome (1981) On the Inapplicability of "Oriental Despotism" and the Asiatic Mode of Production to the Aztecs of Texcoco. *American Antiquity* 46(1), 43–61.

(2010) A Curious Commonality among Some Eastern Basin of Mexico and Eastern Mexican Pictorial Manuscripts. *Estudios de cultura náhuatl* 41, 259–279.

Olson, Mancur (1965) *The Logic of Collective Action: Public Goods and the Theory of Groups*. Cambridge, MA: Harvard University Press.

Onyx, Jenny, and Paul Bullen (2000) Measuring Social Capital in Five Communities. *The Journal of Applied Behavioral Science* 36(1), 23–42.

Oosthuizen, Susan (2013) Beyond Hierarchy: The Archaeology of Collective Governance. *World Archaeology* 45(5), 714–729.

Ortman, Scott G., Andrew H. F. Cabaniss, Jennie O. Sturm, and Luís M. A. Bettencourt (2014) The Pre-History of Urban Scaling. *PloS One* 9(2), e87902.

O'Shea, John M., Ashley K. Lemke, Elizabeth P. Sonnenburg, Robert G. Reynolds, and Brian D. Abbott (2014) A 9,000-Year-Old Caribou Hunting Structure beneath Lake Huron. *Proceedings of the National Academy of Sciences* 111(19), 6911–6915.

Ostrom, Elinor (1990) *Governing the Commons: The Evolution of Institutions for Collective Action*. New York: Cambridge University Press.

(1998) A Behavioral Approach to the Rational Choice Theory of Collective Action: Presidential Address, American Political Science Association, 1997. *American Political Science Review* 92(1), 1–22.

(2000) Collective Action and the Evolution of Social Norms. *The Journal of Economic Perspectives* 14(3), 137–158.

(2005) *Understanding Institutional Diversity*. Princeton, NJ: Princeton University Press.

(2007) Collective Action Theory. In *The Oxford Handbook of Comparative Politics*, edited by Carles Boix and Susan C. Stokes, pp. 186–208. New York: Oxford University Press.

(2009) A General Framework for Analyzing Sustainability of Socio-Ecological Systems. *Science* 325(5939), 419–421.

Ostrom, Elinor, Roy Gardner, and James M. Walker (1994) *Rules, Games, and Common-Pool Resources*. Ann Arbor: University of Michigan Press.

Ostrom, Elinor, Roy Gardner, and James M. Walker (eds.) (2003) *Trust and Reciprocity: Interdisciplinary Lessons from Experimental Research.* New York: Russell Sage Foundation.

Paga, Jessica (2017) Coordination Problems, Common Knowledge, and Architectural Agency: The Case of the Old Bouleuterion in the Athenian Agora. In *Theory in Ancient Greek Archaeology: Manipulating Material Culture in the First Millennium B.C.E.*, edited by Lisa C. Nevett, pp. 189–211. Ann Arbor: University of Michigan Press.

Palka, Joel W. (2023) Ancestral Maya Domesticated Waterscapes, Ecological Aquaculture, and Integrated Subsistence. *Ancient Mesoamerica*, https://doi.org/10.1017/S0956536122000402.

Parsons, Jeffrey R. (2008) Beyond Santley and Rose (1979): The Role of Aquatic Resources in the Prehispanic Economy of the Basin of Mexico. *Journal of Anthropological Research* 64(3), 351–366.

Pastrana Flores, Miguel (2020) La entrega del poder de Motecuhzoma: Una propuesta crítica. *Estudios de Historia Novohispana*, 62, 111–144

Paulinyi, Zoltan (1981) Capitals in Pre-Aztec Central Mexico. *Acta Orientalia Academiae Scientiarum Hungaricae* 35(2/3), 315–350.

Pérez Rodríguez, Veronica (2016) Terrace Agriculture in the Mixteca Alta Region, Oaxaca, Mexico: Ethnographic and Archeological Insights on Terrace Construction and Labor Organization. *Culture, Agriculture, Food and Environment* 38(1), 18–27.

Plunket, Patricia, and Gabriela Uruñuela (2018) *Cholula.* Mexico City: Fondo de Cultura Económica and Colegio de México.

Pohl, John (1994) *The Politics of Symbolism in the Mixtec Codices.* Nashville, TN: Vanderbilt University Press.

Pöllath, Nadja, Oliver Dietrich, Jens Notroff et al. (2018) Almost a Chest Hit: An Aurochs Humerus with Hunting Lesion from Göbekli Tepe, South-Eastern Turkey, and Its Implications. *Quaternary International* 495, 30–48.

Putnam, Robert D., Robert Leonardi, and Rafaella Y. Nanetti (1993) *Making Democracy Work: Civic Traditions in Modern Italy.* Princeton, NJ: Princeton University Press.

Redfield, Robert, and Alfonso Villa Rojas (1967) *Chan Kom: A Maya Village.* Abridged ed., 3rd impression. Chicago, IL: Phoenix Books, University of Chicago Press.

Restall, Matthew, and Wolfgang Gabbert (2017) Maya Ethnogenesis and Group Identity in Yucatan, 1500–1900. In *"The Only True People": Linking Maya Identities Past and Present*, edited by Bethany J. Beyyett and Lisa J. LeCount, pp. 91–130. Boulder: University Press of Colorado.

Restall, Matthew, and Travis Meyer (2023) Personal communication regarding translation of the term "yacatl" to Carballo, March 1, 2023.

Reyes, Daniel Alatorre (2020) El rito para acceder al rango de tecuhtli entre los tlaxcaltecas. *Desacatos: Revista de Ciencias Sociales* 62, 114–129.

Rhodes, Peter J. (2009) Civic Ideology and Citizenship. In *A Companion to Greek and Roman Political History*, edited by Ryan K. Balot, pp. 57–69. Oxford: Blackwell.

Robin, Cynthia (2013) *Everyday Life Matters: Maya Farmers at Chan*. Gainesville: University Press of Florida.

Robinne, François, and Mandy Sadan (eds.) (2007) *Social Dynamics in the Highlands of Southeast Asia: Reconsidering Political Systems of Highland Burma by E. R. Leach*. New York: Brill.

Rojas Rabiela, Teresa (1977) La organización del trabajo para las obras públicas: el coatequitl y las cuadrillas de trabajadores. In *El trabajo y los trabajadores en la historia de México/Labor and Laborers through Mexican History*, edited by Elsa Cecilia Frost, Michael C. Meyer, Josefina Zoraida Vázquez, and Lilia Díaz, pp. 41–66. Tucson and Mexico City: University of Arizona Press and El Colegio de México.

(1986) El sistema de organización en cuadrillas. In *Origen y Formación el Estado en Mesoamérica*, edited by Andrés Medina, Alfredo López Austín, and Mari Carmen Serra, pp. 135–150. Mexico City: Universidad Nacional Autónoma de México.

Rojas Rabiela, Teresa, José Luis Martínez Ruiz, and Daniel Murillo Licea (2009) *Cultura hidráulica y simbolismo mesoamericano del agua en el México prehispánico*. Mexico City: Instituto Mexicano de Tecnología del Agua/Centro de Investigaciones y Estudios Superiores en Antropología Social.

Sahagún, Bernardino de (1997) *Primeros Memoriales*. Paleography of Nahuatl Text and English Translation by Thelma D. Sullivan. Norman: University of Oklahoma Press.

Sanders, William T., Jeffrey R. Parsons, and Robert S. Santley (eds.) (1979) *The Basin of Mexico: Ecological Processes in the Evolution of a Civilization*. New York: Academic Press.

Savage, Mike (2021) *The Return of Inequality: Social Change and the Weight of the Past*. Cambridge, MA: Harvard University Press.

Scarborough, Vernon L., Nicholas P. Dunning, Kenneth B. Tankersley et al. (2012) Water and Sustainable Land Use at the Ancient Tropical City of Tikal, Guatemala. *Proceedings of the National Academy of Sciences* 109(31), 12408–12413.

Schroeder, Susan (1991) *Chimalpahin and the Kingdoms of Chalco*. Tucson: University of Arizona Press.

Scott, James (2009) *The Art of Not Being Governed: An Anarchist History of Upland Southeast Asia*. New Haven, CT: Yale University Press.

Serra Puche, Mari Carmen, Jesús Carlos Lazcano Arce, and Manuel de la Torre Mendoza (2004) Explotación prehipánica de recursos en el sur del valle de Tlaxcala: una perspectiva de género. In *Género, ritual y desarrollo sostenido en comunidades rurales de Tlaxcala*, edited by Pilar Alberti Manzanares, pp. 199–226. Mexico City: Colegio de Postgraduados, Barcelona, and Plaza y Valdés.

Sharif, Hasan (2012) The Day Dr. King Visited Boston Common in 1965. *The Bay State Banner*, January 10. www.baystatebanner.com/2012/01/10/the-day-dr-king-visited-boston-common-in-1965-3/.

Small, David B. (2009) The Dual-Processual Model in Ancient Greece: Applying a Post-Neoevolutionary Model to a Data-Rich Environment. *Journal of Anthropological Archaeology* 28, 205–221.

Smith, Michael E. (2015) The Aztec Empire. In *Fiscal Regimes and the Political Economy of Premodern States*, edited by Andrew Monson and Walter Scheidel, pp. 71–114. New York: Cambridge University Press.

Smith, Monica L. (2016) Urban Infrastructure as Materialized Consensus. *World Archaeology* 48(1), 164–178.

Sökefeld, Martin (1999) Debating Self, Identity, and Culture in Anthropology. *Current Anthropology* 40(4), 417–448.

Šprajc, Ivan, Takeshi Inomata, and Anthony F. Aveni (2023) Origins of Mesoamerican Astronomy and Calendar: Evidence from the Olmec and Maya Regions. *Science Advances* 9, eabq767.

Spres, Ronald, and Andrew K. Balkansky (2013) *The Mixtecs of Oaxaca: Ancient Times to the Present*. Norman: University of Oklahoma Press.

Stanish, Charles (2017) *The Evolution of Human Cooperation*. New York: Cambridge University Press.

Sugiyama, Saburo, and Leonardo López Luján (2007) Dedicatory Burial/Offering Complexes at the Moon Pyramid, Teotihuacan: A Preliminary Report of 1998–2004 Explorations. *Ancient Mesoamerica* 18, 127–146.

Thompson, Victor D. (2022) Considering Ideas of Collective Action, Institutions, and "Hunter-Gatherers" in the American Southeast. *Journal of Archaeological Research*, https://doi.org/10.1007/s10814-022-09179-3.

Thompson, Victor D., Jacob Holland-Lulewicz, RaeLynn A. Butler et al. (2022) The Early Materialization of Democratic Institutions among the Ancestral Muskogean of the American Southeast. *American Antiquity* 87(4), 704–723.

Thompson, Victor D., William H. Marquardt, Karen J. Walker, Amanda D. Roberts Thompson, and Lee A. Newsom (2018) Collective Action, State Building, and the Rise of the Calusa, Southwest Florida, USA. *Journal of Anthropological Archaeology* 51, 28–44.

Thurston, Tina L. (2022) Reversals of Fortune: Shared Governance, "Democracy," and Reiterated Problem-Solving. *Frontiers in Political Science* 4, 870773.

Turchin, Peter, Thomas E. Currie, Edward A. L. Turner, and Sergey Gavrilets (2013) War, Space, and the Evolution of Old World Complex Societies. *Proceedings of the National Academy of Sciences* 110(41), 16384–16389.

Turner, Andrew D., and Michael D. Mathiowetz (2021) Introduction. Flower Worlds: A Synthesis and Critical History. In *Flower Worlds: Religion, Aesthetics, and Ideology in Mesoamerica and the American Southwest*, edited by Michael D. Mathiowetz and Andrew D. Turner, pp. 3–34. Tucson: University of Arizona Press.

Turner, B. L., and Peter D. Harrison (2000) Pulltrouser Swamp and Maya Raised Fields: A Summation. In *Pulltrouser Swamp: Ancient Maya Habitat, Agriculture, and Settlement in Northern Belize*, edited by B. L. Turner and Peter D. Harrison, pp. 246–270. Salt Lake City: University of Utah Press.

UN-Habitat (2020) *The New Urban Agenda Illustrated*. Nairobi: United Nations Human Settlements Programme (UN-Habitat).

van Zantwijk, Rudolph (1985) *The Aztec Arrangement: The Social History of Pre-Spanish Mexico*. Norman: University of Oklahoma Press.

Whittaker, Gordon (2021) *Deciphering Aztec Hieroglyphs: A Guide to Nahuatl Writing*. Oakland: University of California Press.

Widgren, Mats (2007). Pre-Colonial Landesque Capital: A Global Perspective. In *Rethinking Environmental History: World-System History and Global Environmental Change*, edited by Alf Hornborg, J. R. McNeill, and Joan Martínez-Alier, pp. 61–77. Lanham, MD: AltaMira Press.

Wilken, Gene C. (1968) Drained-Field Agriculture: An Intensive Farming System in Tlaxcala, Mexico. *The Geographical Review* 59(2), 215–241.

Winter, Marcus, and Teresa Alarcón (2021) The Preceramic in Oaxaca. In *Preceramic Mesoamerica*, edited by Jon C. Lohse, Aleksander Borejsza, and Arthur A. Joyce, pp. 304–327. New York: Routledge.

Wylie, Alison (1985) The Reaction Against Analogy. *Advances in Archaeological Method and Theory* 8, 63–111.

Yue, Xiahe, Anne Antonietti, Mitra Alirezaei et al. (2022) Using Convolutional Neural Networks to Derive Neighborhood Built Environments from Google Street View Images and Examine Their Associations with Health

Outcomes. *International Journal of Environmental Research and Public Health* 19(19), 12095.

Zorita, Alonso de (1963) *Life and Labor in Ancient Mexico: The Brief and Summary Relation of the Lords of New Spain.* Translated by Benjamin Keen. New Brunswick, NJ: Rutgers University Press.

# Acknowledgments

We are grateful to Rita Wright and John Millhauser for their gracious assistance in shepherding this Element to press and to two anonymous reviewers for comments on how to improve its previous incarnation. We thank Joe Bagley and Brandeis University Press for assistance in obtaining rights to the Boston Common cowbell depicted in Figure 1; Matthew Restall and Travis Meyer for their thoughts on the etymology of the Nahuatl term tlayacatl; Marcelo Canuto for the map of Pulltrowser Swamp in Figure 15; Jim Neely for comments relating to the Purrón Dam Complex; and Tony Aveni for comments relating to pecked crosses. All errors in interpreting their research are ours.

Cambridge Elements ≡

# Anthropological Archaeology in the 21st Century

## Eli Dollarhide

*New York University Abu Dhabi*

Eli Dollarhide is an archaeological anthropologist who specializes in the prehistory of the Middle East with a focus on the Persian Gulf. His research investigates the role of small and rural settlements in the development of Bronze Age exchange networks and political systems. Dollarhide co-directs research at the UNESCO World Heritage Site of Bat, Oman and investigates ancient ceramic technologies. See: https://nyuad.nyu.edu/en/research/faculty-labs-and-projects/humanities-research-fellowship-program/research-fellows/eli-dollarhide.html.

## Michael Galaty

*University of Michigan*

Michael Galaty is Professor of Anthropology in the Department of Anthropology and Director and Curator of European and Mediterranean Archaeology in the Museum of Anthropological Archaeology at the University of Michigan. He conducts fieldwork in Albania, Greece, and Kosovo, with a focus on the prehistoric origins of social inequalities. To that end, he utilizes intensive regional survey and targeted excavations, along with various laboratory techniques, to track the changing economic and political factors that lead to transformative changes in Mediterranean and Balkan social systems, during the Bronze Age, in particular, mgalaty@umich.edu.

## Junko Habu

*University of California, Berkeley*

Junko Habu is Professor of Anthropology and Chair of the Center for Japanese Studies, University of California, Berkeley, and Affiliate Professor of the Research Institute for Humanity and Nature. She has published extensively on Japanese and East Asian archaeology, hunter-gatherer archaeology and historical ecology. Her current research focuses on the intersection of archeology, agroecology and traditional ecological knowledge to consider the resilience of socioeconomic systems in the past, present and future. For more information, see https://junkohabu.com/

## Patricia A. McAnany

*University of North Carolina at Chapel Hill*

Patricia A. McAnany, Kenan Eminent Professor and Chair of Anthropology at the University of North Carolina at Chapel Hill, is co-director of Proyecto Arqueológico Colaborativo del Oriente de Yucatán – a community-archaeology project at Tahcabo, Yucatán, México. She co-founded and directs InHerit: Indigenous Heritage Passed to Present (www.in-herit.org) a UNC program that generates collaborative research and education projects focused on archaeology and cultural heritage with communities in the Maya region and North Carolina. She is the author of several books (most recently Maya Cultural Heritage: How Archaeologists and Indigenous Peoples Engage the Past) as well as journal articles and book chapters on a range of archaeological and heritage topics.

## John K. Millhauser

*North Carolina State University*
John K. Millhauser is an Associate Professor of Anthropology in the Department of Sociology and Anthropology at North Carolina State University. His archaeological work in Mexico centers on rural communities and social economies under Mexica and Spanish rule. His current research integrates economic anthropology and political ecology to better understand the origins of poverty and structural violence. For more information, visit chass. ncsu.edu/people/jkmillha/

## Rita Wright

*New York University*
Rita Wright, Professor Emerita of Anthropology at New York University. Using Near Eastern texts as secondary sources and ancient technologies (ceramics and weaving), she investigates divisions of labor and women's contributions to history. In the field she has conducted research in Afghanistan, Pakistan, and Iran, predominately in Baluchistan at Mehrgarh and the Punjab, Pakistan, at the city of Harappa. Her Landscape and Settlement survey of Harappa's rural areas is the first conducted in studies of the Indus civilization. She is founder and editor of Cambridge University Press, Case Studies in Early Societies, especially Ancient Indus: Urbanism, Economy, and Society (Cambridge University Press, 2010); rpw2@nyu.edu.

---

## About the Series

This Element offers anthropological and contemporary perspectives in the study of prehistoric and historic societies globally and cutting-edge research with balanced coverage of well-known sites and understudied times and places. We solicit contributions based on three themes: 1. new methods and technologies producing fresh understandings of the past; 2. theoretical approaches challenging basic concepts and offering new insights; 3. archaeological responses for the 21st century providing informed choices for the present. Individual volumes focus on specific sites and regions that highlight the diversity of human experience around the world and across history which include scholars working throughout North America, Mesoamerica, Europe and the Mediterranean, Africa, the Middle East, and South and East Asia and readers with an avid interest in the latest frontiers in archaeological thought. The media-rich volumes will be an important resource for students, scholars.

**Cambridge Elements** ☰

# Anthropological Archaeology in the 21st Century

## Elements in the Series

*Collective Action and the Reframing of Early Mesoamerica*
David M. Carballo and Gary M. Feinman

A full series listing is available at: www.cambridge.org/EATF

Printed in the United States
by Baker & Taylor Publisher Services